Golf
Against
Cancer

Golf Against Cancer

A Month of Madness on the M25

Trevor Sandford

To order additional copies of this book, contact:
Xlibris Corporation
0-800-644-6988
www.xlibrispublishing.co.uk
Orders@xlibrispublishing.co.uk
303542

Contents

The GAC Tour:
A Month of Madness on the M25

Life After the Tour

For one in three of us

Acknowledgements

When you play golf for a month you don't always have time for a "p" so I have saved them all up here. Thanks to Diana for provision of pasties; to Ian for publicity, PR, persistence, photographs and persuading me to keep going; to Andy for putting prowess in our pairs partnership and for putting the past behind him; to John for pre-eminent participation and philanthropy. Thanks to all golf club secretaries and club professionals for their preparation and prompt support; to all publications which promoted the project and all the people who pledged or played in this pan-London pantomime. Thanks to Payden's Pharmacy for (ibu) profen and preventative podiatry products and for the press and publicity provided by the following: *The Social Golfer, Cancer Research UK, Today's Golfer, Golf Monthly, Golf News, The Downsmail, The Kent Messenger, The Sunday Mirror, The Times, BBC Radio Kent, Essex and Berkshire.*

Photographs by the author and his playing partners except Peter Erlam, *The Downs Mail* (front cover); Ian Mullins, *The Social Golfer* (rear cover & background, pp 18,36,48); John Amos(p 173); Heather Parker (p 112), Kevin Frid (p178).

Preface

This is not a book about golf. I hope golfers will enjoy reading it but so also, I hope, will saxophonists, sign-writers and secretaries. Wives and daughters get the occasional mention, though not husbands and sons, but only because I don't have any of these. Motorway drivers and their passengers will find it of some interest, as will takers of Ibuprofen. Anyone who knows anyone who has ever had a pain in their shoulder will find light relief within these pages. You will not find an apostrophe out of place in this book, though people who like quotation marks should look away now. School subjects covered herein include English, maths, science, geography, history, languages, PE, RE and home economics. However this book does not have the official endorsement of the Education Secretary and will, unfortunately, not help you with your GCSEs.

This book also contains accounts of particular challenges which should not be tried at home. Please note that any mention of driving on the hard shoulder should not be interpreted literally; as we all know, putting is much more suitable on a flat surface. Also, the opinions expressed within these pages are not necessarily those of the author and have been included purely for dramatic effect. Any person feeling that they can recognise themselves here and have been unfairly represented should consider changing their name.

Any invitations to participate in all-expenses-paid corporate golfing events or foreign travel should be sent to the author. Law suits will be dealt with by Mr I Mullins of *The Social Golfer* whose assurances I have in writing. For everyone else, if you enjoy reading this half as much as I enjoyed doing it, I shall be a happy man.

Trevor Sandford

Hard Shoulder, M25

December 2011

The Project

We've all been there

It's the biggest car-park in the world. We've all been stuck on it. We've all tried to avoid it. We've all wondered whether the outside lane really is faster. We've found it was—until we pushed our way into it and then it stopped. We've thought we should have left earlier. We've looked at those other people in the Ford Galaxy. Are they on the Uni run too? No, they're moving house, they must be with all that stuff. No, they're going on a camping holiday. Well they'll never make the ferry. How long is it to the services? Are we nearly there? Can we have an ice-cream? I need the toilet. Can I do it here? It's no good, I can't wait any longer. That man's picking his nose. Well he could have picked a better one.

We've all been there

Actually, as in love, so in life: we're all pretty unkind to our dearest, closest friend. We take her for granted and complain about all her faults. But just think what life was like before the M25. Maidstone to Guildford in an hour—you must be joking. Gatwick to Stansted—don't even think about it. Bristol to Cambridge—pack an overnight bag. Now the 172 mile Uni run from Kent to Nottingham takes less than 3 hours—courtesy of the M20/M2, the M1 and, of course, at the heart of it all, the M25. We couldn't do without it. And as for the trip to the mother-in-law's in Dorset, well without the M25 you can forget it. And good thing too say the people of Dorking . . . or Brentwood . . . or Rickmansworth. It just wasn't possible to get around London in the olden days. Well, OK, we had the North Circular, the A412 and so on (the South Circular has never existed in my book and, not being circular, is anyway a complete misnomer) but you couldn't really get around London without adding either miles or hours to your journey. Now you can. Well, OK, sometimes. Actually most times, though it never seems to feel that way.

Doing something crazy

Why do we do crazy things? What is it that drives us to abseiling with an ironing board or running the London marathon dressed like a banana? Because it's there? Well, that's OK up to a point. Everest *is* there, was there, will be there next week. But to say you've climbed it—that's all about challenge and achievement. I was always going to climb Kilimanjaro myself (actually, it's a decent walk for a fit person with the right gear and preparation) but once the celebs got to it in 2009 it was somehow, for me, tarnished. It wouldn't have been *my* idea any more. And that's the second thing—something *I've* done, something self-affirming, top of Maslow's hierarchy and all that, something to write on my epitaph, something that marks me out. And of course nowadays how do you stand out? When everyone has done it before, you have only 2 options—do it faster or do it different. So, unless you are an elite athlete, looking for a place in the record books, it's doing it different—hence the banana, or the diving-suit, or the ironing board, or whatever. Golf on the M25 even.

On top of this, we all want to make a difference. There is so much going on in the world, if I am going to do something crazy I might as well do it *for* something: the higher cause; the deeper motivation; something bigger than myself. That's what it's all about. So it has to be a fundraiser, a big charity reflecting the scale of the task: worthy effort for a worthy cause; grand, cleansing, aspirational, spiritual . . . So the banana serves a greater end and everybody wins.

The power of numbers

Did anybody notice there were 31 junctions on the M25? Maybe it was just me. I do have 2 O-levels, 2 A-levels and half a degree in Maths, so I suppose I've always been taken by numbers. I used to prevent boredom as I cycled to school by adding up car number-plates to see what they came to. Not possible these days with so many letters so we make up acronyms instead. (GL54 HML = Good luck hogging middle lane etc) And yes, I do occasionally watch *Countdown* ("one from the top and five small numbers, please, Rachel"). I can't actually say when the penny dropped on the motorway itself that there were 31 junctions and, since there were 31 days in a month (mostly), you could do something every day around the M25. I was probably counting down the junctions to the Dartford crossing going clockwise and wondering why the traffic was so much faster in the other direction, but somehow the numbers matched up and the seed of the month of golf was sown. By the way, I did finish my degree—the other half was physics. And, yes, I do know about junction 21A.

Why golf?

Why not? It's what I do. I'm not a runner, I'm a golfer. It's how I've spent my Saturday mornings since I first got hooked about 12 years ago. It's about exercise, challenge, camaraderie, banter, friendship, competition, stress relief, getting out of the house, all of that. Ask any golfer why they play—there's a host of reasons. Fine, but golf *on the M25?* Yes, that's the banana/ironing-board thing, I suppose. Two completely unconnected things that suddenly combined reveal a whole new world of possibilities. Like the great paradigm shifts in scientific discovery, you might say. Well, let's not get carried away, it was probably the much more mundane fact that you do pass a few golf courses on the motorway and, after a fleeting glance, might think "that looks a nice track" or "wouldn't fancy playing there right up against the motorway" or "aren't we near Wentworth here?"

Enter Google Maps. Zoom in on the M25, type in golf clubs and the place is peppered with pink dots. Turns out there are about 140 clubs within 5 miles of the motorway, including some prestigious household names. What about playing one of those every day as you make your way around the world largest roundabout? Magic!

Why now?

Dream on, mate. When would I get the time—or the cash—to do that? You're talking 31 days here. Sounds like a retirement project and that's a long way off. Or so I thought. There have been many unexpected outcomes of the economic downturn, not many of them good. But going suddenly from full-on up to London every day on the train to sitting around home in the autumn of 2010 did give some cause for a rethink. People respond to a sudden change in their work life in a number of ways and that's a whole new subject. One minute you are complaining you haven't got time to do anything, you are far too busy and then suddenly you can't say that anymore. You now have the opportunity. Well, why not seize it? What's your excuse? You may be lucky enough to have a bit of cash in the bank and now you're "time-rich", so go for it.

So it was that one Monday in November I sat down at the computer and got to work. A tentative email to a national golf magazine telling them about the project elicited a positive response within the hour. I was away. It was going to happen. 2011 would bring on the Month of Golf.

Why cancer?

Again, as Ian would go on to say later, "sometimes the planets just align . . ." Things feed into your unconscious. I went on a singing day (another stress-relieving spare-time occupation) and found a song written for a Cancer Research service of celebration. Sadly I attended the funeral of a former colleague and it was "donations to Cancer Research UK". Meanwhile my pairs partner and best golfing buddy Andy got hit in the summer—pancreatic, not good. We'd reached the finals of the club summer pairs. On 28th September we had a "last game before the Op"; he gave me 2 shots; I was 6 down after 11 and won the last 7 holes to win 1 up—had I no sympathy? He watched the Ryder Cup from a hospital bed. We were due to go on a golfing break to Vilamoura in October. That didn't happen. Chemotherapy happened instead. Life was on hold. Suddenly the realities of that dreadful disease came close to home. If I needed a worthy cause to support, I didn't have far to look.

So Golf Against Cancer took shape. I'd play my month of golf but I'd do it for a good cause. Nobody I know has been unaffected by cancer via a friend or family member. Everyone has heard of it. Everyone wants to see a cure and relief from life-draining symptoms. Cancer Research UK was happy to have my support. My mate was fighting back to health—we had our final to play, hadn't we? And we want to play *next* summer . . . and the next. We're not going to let this beat us. Game on.

Am I ready for this?

The Plan

It was only a dream then

What do you do between Christmas and New Year? The turkey is all gone, you don't want to see another mince pie, you've played with your new toys, you've been to the sales . . . well, obviously you play golf. And if you can't *play* golf, you can always *think* about golf. You can even *shop* about golf. So it was that I stumbled on the Roger Kidd Golf Guide *50 miles of Golf around London* as I wandered around American Golf looking at all the new gear. This little volume features over 600 courses, shown on a series of maps and with basic info, a one-line description and contact details given for each. Ranging from Silverstone to Sandwich, it more than covered my patch and I spent a happy evening with a glass or two of wine working my way around the M25, making a shortlist of half a dozen courses within easy reach of every junction. Then I put it away in a drawer somewhere. It was a nice idea, but I wasn't really ever going to do it, was I?

Cast your bread upon the waters . . .

Well, that must have been 2009. Now I *had* decided to take the plunge, what did I need to do to make it happen? All those years of senior corporate roles and running my own business must have taught me something. If you fail to plan, you plan to fail etc etc. But where do you start? First of all, it needs dedicated time. I must have spent 2 weeks solid in November getting the whole thing set up. My wife kept asking "are you still on sabbatical?" I couldn't have done it in the evenings and weekends. Second, you couldn't do it without IT. It doesn't actually save you time, it just opens up more possibilities. So you click on the pink dot on Google Maps, then onto the website, or read the reviews, fly over each hole, look at the course map, check out the green fees, try to figure out who to contact—and log it all on the proverbial spreadsheet. Third, you have to remember, no one replies to their emails.

Who'd be a Club secretary?

That's not entirely fair. Some people get back straight away, but a lot never bother. Look at your own inbox. You are up to your eyes in stuff and Email number 43 today arrives:

Dear fellow golfer:

During August 2011, I shall be playing my way around the M25, turning off at a different junction every day to play golf (there are 31 junctions). The trip will raise money for Cancer Research UK and will be covered by Today's Golfer magazine.

I should like to include your club in this event and am looking for a single tee-time for up to 4 players, all of whom will be contributing to the fundraising effort. In view of the charity involved, many clubs have felt able to offer courtesy of the course or in some cases guest rates; this clearly maximises the charity contribution. Courses involved will be publicised via the magazine's website, which is widely visited, and in other publicity material for the event.

Could I ask whether it would be possible to secure a tee-time, what charge would be applicable and whether you have any additional requirements? I am keen to confirm the itinerary in the next week or two as I have a number of courses already pending.

I should like to visit on Wednesday 10th August, ideally perhaps at 11 am, though we can be very flexible. Many thanks for your assistance in this endeavour.

Trevor Sandford, Month of Golf 2011, In support of Cancer Research UK

You are a very efficient, kind-hearted person who recognises effort for a good cause when you see it and you reply:

Dear Trevor

I am happy to offer a complimentary round at Burhill in support of your effort to raise money for Cancer Research on Wednesday 10 August on the New Course. I can confirm I have booked you in at 11am and on arrival, please report to our Pro Shop for course tags.

I wish you every success in your attempt to play the M25 and look forward to you visiting Burhill. If Today's Golfer require any further information from us, we will be happy to accommodate.

Kind regards

Gill

Thank you Gill, you are wonderful. We have never met, but you make my day worthwhile. I just need another 30 like you. I *will* carry on; it's going to happen now.

Follow-up is a full-time job

In the main, however, you can't rely on an email; you have to give them a call. Working out who the key person is can be a real challenge. Golf clubs are so different. Most members' clubs have a secretary, a committee and so on. Some clubs are part of a larger group or a wider leisure enterprise; some are run by the local authority. All have a pro-shop; in the end, the pro is often the best person to speak to, though often it's the secretary or committee who make the decisions, especially if you are after something. One secretary told me mine was the 125th request he had had for support for a charity since the beginning of the year. Another thought I was trying to sell her something. Eventually you get to speak to the right person. When you explain what you are doing and they get it, they are more than helpful. It's amazing what "doing something for a good cause" does to open doors and how amenable most clubs can be when they realise you are not just on the scrounge. But it all takes time and the spreadsheet is looking a little ragged. I set myself the notional target of having everything fixed up by Christmas. By 1st December I have 5 yes's, 3 nos and 2 maybes. Perhaps a week of golf might have been a better idea.

I plough on more in hope than expectation. Caroline is up to her neck in Christmas parties; Kelly will ask Chester; Jo will call me back. All the "no"s have a good reason, often "annual maintenance". So that's what they do in August, then. Weekends are particularly difficult; we could offer you the Monday—I'll be somewhere else then, sorry—but Saturday's wall-to-wall with members—yes, I can appreciate that, what about later in the afternoon—the 8th looks a possibility—no but you are near junction 6, you see, so by then I'll have moved around—you mean you are playing every day yourself—er, yes, that's the idea, it's a month of golf—oh, I see, and you just want one tee-time? Etc, etc Actually most people do get it and by Christmas, I have a pretty good itinerary, with some of the best courses around London happy to offer a complimentary fourball to a complete nutter on the basis that he is raising money for cancer research and doing something absurd in the process.

Where do you draw the line?

When you are planning any project you do have to be clear about your objectives. One of mine was that if I was going to play every day for a month, I wanted to visit some memorable courses. Unfortunately, the Wentworth Club couldn't help, though I did have a personal letter from the chief executive explaining how much they already contributed to charitable causes each year. Sunningdale was unfortunately one of those closed for maintenance. Some sections of the M25 have an embarrassment of riches in terms of the quality of the clubs nearby; others, shall we say, are less well favoured. I'll leave you to guess which. So how do you assess whether it's worth pursuing a particular lead, especially if you haven't played or even heard of the venue? Here the website can be very revealing and a combination of the green-fee, the scorecard, the gallery and the comments can give you the clues you need. Unfortunately there's no comprehensive source of consistent reviews. Some magazines and websites do have them, but it's often "horses for courses" and one man's challenging layout will be another man's open field. I resolve to write a review of every course I play and offer them to the two national magazines I have got interested.

In the end, I'm pretty pleased with the results. I name-drop some of the venues I've got and people are well impressed. I've managed to avoid (I hope) the kind of place you are going to turn up in hope and walk away after a few holes. Nothing too short, no pitch'n'putts in disguise, only one 9 holer (and it looks a good one), a mix of members' clubs and corporate venues and all in all I can't wait to get out there and play. Will anyone join me? Time to think about publicity.

Pushing the boat out.

Colin, my friend, IT guru and occasional golfing partner runs me up a little flyer on the computer. I send it out to a few friends. I proudly print them off and carry them around with me. *Today's Golfer* put a nice little feature in their new year magazine; *Golf Monthly* give it a mention in their April edition. I get some stuff from Cancer Research UK. I set up a web-page on *JustGiving*. I send out Emails to former colleagues. People start giving money. Wow! I mean not golfy people, just people who know me and *know* I'm crazy. Now I feel responsible. I mustn't let them down. Not only will I have to do it, I'll have to make a proper job of it.

Friends, Romans, countrymen . . .

Trouble is, so far, I'll be doing it on my own—well that's the great worry. Nobody else is stupid enough to want to play golf for a month. But they might do a week, or just a day even. That would be good. Let's see, 31x3=93. Yikes, I've got nearly 100 slots I can fill. I've set myself a target to raise at least £100/day, so I'd better get out there and get some of my golfing buddies on board. I send out the email flyer, I tell people at the club, we talk about it after a game. Everyone is well impressed. Of course, they'll come and join me. Thing is, though, they haven't really sorted their holidays yet, so they can't really say. I am going to have to be patient—and persistent—and promotional too if I'm not going to tread the fairways like Billy no-mates.

You can get anything on the internet nowadays

A few years ago, Colin came to me with a business proposition—a "find somebody to play with" golf website. I wonder if anyone else has thought of it, so I go surfing to find out. I find loads: findagolfpartner. com, igolf, golfmates, teeoffbuddies, golf-finder, vgs, golfshake, teefortwo and more. I start putting my details up on one—you generally have to register to get more info. I say my handicap, my club, how often I play, how wide an area etc. That's all fine. Then it asks about height, colour of hair, other hobbies etc and I begin to feel a bit uncomfortable—what was this site called? Well you put partner into a search engine and what do you expect? At least the wife wasn't looking. In the end I register on a couple, or at least I think I have, it's hard to tell sometimes, turn off the computer and go off to bed, dreaming of strolling down the fairways with some gorgeous 10-handicapper until the clear light of morning dawns.

The Partnership

Hi Trevor,

I hope you don't mind me contacting you directly but I stumbled across your 'Month of Golf' group posting over the weekend and was very interested in your project. And I couldn't help wondering if this is not something that we could help you with a little more than just finding you some members to join you in your odyssey?

I hope you don't mind me asking but would you be interesting in meeting up to discuss further at some stage before not to long?

Look forward to hearing from you.

Warm Regards

Ian Mullins
Managing Director
The TSG Team

Suddenly on 8th March, I get this email from *The Social Golfer*. So there is a real person behind this website—and he is interested in my project. Just how interested I'd find out in due course, but for now, yes, why not meet up and see. Turns out he's in Essex, I'm in Kent, so where do we meet? Just off the M25, by the Dartford crossing.

I find the hotel which is our designated meeting place and think: why would anyone want to stay here, with a view of the toll-booths as you pull back the curtains, but somebody must as the place is big enough. Then I find I have to pay 3 quid to park. Groan. Fair enough, I suppose, otherwise it'd be full of Kent car-sharers working in Essex avoiding the toll or whatever. I go in, find the bar, sit somewhere obvious with a golf mag and wait. Ian arrives. Actually he recognises me from my profile picture on the website so I didn't need the golf mag. I buy him a drink. £3.15 for a diet coke. These are West End prices and were in . . . Dartford! Anyway, I recover my composure and get down to the meeting.

Have you ever had that feeling when you come up with an idea and suddenly find someone else picking it up and running with it? Research scientists must get it all the time, but there's a kind of buzz when someone else picks up your baby and goes goo goo at it and over the next half hour, out poured a host of ideas from this man's fertile brain. From a background in marketing, he'd taken over this "Facebook for Golf" website. He was taken by my plans and felt they could fill all my games with his members. More than that, it could be their flagship project. He had media contacts who could promote it. What was my fundraising target—we could double it. What was next year's project—a month of golf round the world? He had contacts at Emirates Airways . . .

Whoa, hang on, now. This is *my* project, not some new product going to market. Still you are making me an offer here, of time, expertise, investment, enthusiasm. Why wouldn't I run with it? So somehow the beginnings of a partnership were seeded over a diet coke and I began to see a wider world of opportunities, knew that two heads would be better than one and wondered where it would all lead. As I waited to pay for my parking and get out of the hotel, I noticed it was £14.75 for continental breakfast. I wouldn't be turning off here again on my trip around the M25 but it was the birthplace of Golf Against Cancer—a month of madness on the M25.

Sometimes the planets just align

There are only six degrees of separation between all of us, they say, so throw in a couple of key links and that comes down to two or three. Turns out that Ian used to work for MediaCom and Cancer Research UK was one of their clients. He's off playing golf with his former boss soon so he'll drop it in the conversation. Then he goes to the City Am editor who says he'll mention it to his cousin. Who's his cousin? Sam Torrance. And so on. Once the wheels start turning, you see links you hadn't expected or even thought of.

And here's another one. I'd been thinking for a while I need to set up a website, get a blog going, start tweeting. Trouble is, I'm not really a Facebook person; more LinkedIn, me. But that's very much a business thing. You can state your interests but that's not really what it's for. Here now I have a ready-made website that's prepared to let me blog away about my adventures—what's not to like? Then I start thinking whether I need a new laptop, whether golf clubs have wi-fi, whether Premier Inn would sponsor me and lots more to keep me awake.

Hammering out the detail

A bit like dating, it's the second meet-up that counts. The first may be a bit starry-eyed, but then you have to hammer out how (or whether) things are going to work. I send Ian the Email:

> *Ian*
>
> *It was very good to meet you last week. I was touched by the way you have responded to my idea and impressed by the range of possibilities that you have suggested. I should definitely like to work in partnership over the next few months to develop some of them in a way that will add value to our different enterprises and produce a resource for a good cause. I am happy to move*

sooner rather than later on the details now but we would need to hammer out what those entail.

Trevor

We arrange to meet up at the golf club where I finish my odyssey—it's on the Essex side so my turn to pay the toll. We meet the secretary's assistant who gives us an info pack. We have a good chat with the pro, who, like everyone else, is really taken with what I am up to. We meet the Captain who's happy to help, we chat for hours as the sun goes down on a lovely golf course—and we don't get to play! I do, however, have a massive piece of sponge cake and tea for very little money and I can see the "Golfer's guide to eating and drinking around the M25" already shaping up. Ian says we need a powerpoint (for marketing purposes) and talks about "branding" but he is so enthusiastic I can forgive him for both of these extravagant suggestions.

The Project Team

Minor celebrity ensues

Within a couple of weeks we have all the info ready to launch and he has contacted City AM, The Evening Standard, Sport Magazine, The Economist & Business Week. So far all the feedback has been positive with Business Week, City AM and hopefully The Evening Standard interested in meeting up. The assistant sports editor of the Daily Mirror thought it was a great idea and we talk about getting Chris Evans involved—he's a golf nut who would recognise a crazy idea when he sees it. Meanwhile, back in humble Bearsted, Kent, my mate's friend happens to be the deputy editor of the Downs Mail, a wonderful local free paper that goes to every home around Maidstone. We nip down to my local club where he snaps me in a golf buggy and we chat over a cup of tea. Next week it's on the front page in full colour. People from the tennis club have seen it. Somebody I hardly know gives me a donation. I don't exactly have to wear a hoodie and dark glasses to go shopping but I have that sense of minor celebrity status I last enjoyed over 30 years ago when I toured in a support band with Cliff Richard. No, honest, I did. Really. And that's Chris Evans and Cliff Richard in the same paragraph—how did that happen?

Golf and Cancer—a curious partnership

It's May now and I get an intriguing Email from a 75-year old who plays off 7 and has written a golf instruction book for amateurs whilst on chemotherapy. He's donating the proceeds to Cancer Research too, so we have a chat about how we can help each other out. I suggest meeting up for a game of golf (he's a member at Royal Ashdown Forest and I fancy playing there . . .) but unfortunately he can't play at the moment. Oh, yes, of course, how thoughtless of me. Oh, no, it's not the cancer or anything, he fell on the golf course and broke his shoulder a few weeks ago, but he'll be OK by the summer. George Rothman seems a remarkable person; I invite him to join me in August. Maybe we could play at Surrey Downs—it's a Peter Alliss design and

Peter has done the foreword for his book. Maybe he'll come and play too? Hey, why not, you can always ask.

And then Seve died. 7 May 2011. A legend. An inspiration. On the course or in the hospital bed. He was always a fighter and left such a mark on the world of golf. From inspiring countless youngsters to take up the game to putting Europe where it is at the top of world golf, his influence has been immense. I holidayed in Tenerife the week before and paid my own personal tribute by driving nearly 2 hours to Buenavista to play the course he designed there, set right up against the ocean. Aren't there any nearer courses, my wife asked innocently. Yes, but they're not Seve courses. She hasn't a clue what I'm on about but a golfer will know at once. I'm playing The Shire in the summer, his only UK project. We'll have to do something special.

The Preparation

In my first summer at university, I worked in a kids' camp in America. I had a great time, earned some money and travelled through 25 states in the month before coming home. I remember filling in the forms the winter before I went. They were quite straightforward until it came to one question: Can you swim 25 metres? Actually, being USA, it was probably yards. Anyway, I grew up 45 miles from the seaside, there was no local swimming pool, the river was "too dangerous" and neither of my parents swam. So on those rare days to the seaside, I paddled and made sand-castles like everyone else. I'd panic if I waded in beyond my thighs. What was I going to do? Well, motivation is everything, so I ticked the "yes" box, went down to the municipal baths and bought myself a season ticket. The first visit was scary, the second ugly and on the third, people knew to avoid me as I splashed the five strokes across the pool vaguely copying other people but with a lot more energy and a lot less momentum. Anyway, when summer arrived I could swim the requisite 25 metres, loved diving and wanted to snorkel. When I got to the camp, I discovered they actually had a lifeguard, but hey if I'd known that I might never have learned to swim.

So now I'm looking ahead and thinking: can you play every day for a month? Well, as before I just ticked the "yes" box and plunged in. This year I would need very little excuse to get out and play golf. A few years before, I'd started keeping a record of my rounds and I'd been playing maybe 80-90 a year—an average of about 2 a week. This year it'll be well over 100. Any chance of playing I took up—especially 36 holes a day. If I could play five rounds over a long weekend, I'd be getting nearer to the target I'd set myself and perhaps one round a day wouldn't feel so bad after all. I'd need to work on fitness, of course, and then there'd be general wear and tear. I bought a couple of extra pairs of golf shoes, so I could wear a different pair on consecutive days, helping to reduce blistering (I reckoned—though maybe just one pair of very well-fitting shoes would be enough?) I thought about wearing a glove on *both* hands. I could always take a buggy, but somehow that'd be cheating—you have to walk the course to say you've been there. Most importantly, I'd have to learn to play within myself.

Mens sana

I really took up golf properly only about 10 years ago. I've progressed from a starting handicap of 28 down to 12 or so in various jumps. I'm also the oldest amongst the group of guys I play with most Saturday mornings. Yet I can hit it further than most of them. Well, sometimes, anyway. Ok, all right, *once* then—and yes we did have wind behind . . . Still when you have leathered it over 300 yards and are looking at a short iron to the green rather than another great thump, it is very tempting to try to do it every time. So I'm trying to larrop it off every tee and it's not doing wonders for my game—let alone my back. And I'm also doing quite a bit of wandering off piste looking for the ball. I can't keep this up for a month; I'll have to learn to play more conservatively.

My club pro kindly offers me a couple of complimentary lessons, as I'm doing this for charity, so we go down the range and he says how can I help. Well where do I start? I'm trying to murder it off the tee, my irons are a bit inconsistent, I can't hit a fairway wood for toffee and I'm struggling to get out of bunkers. Oh, my putting isn't too bad though. Well we hit a few balls and he gives me some useful tips to avoid overswinging and steepen my angle of attack, so it should all be a bit crisper and more controlled; now I need to practice! I also need plenty of good swing thoughts like "make it to the finish" and stuff like that. I may need a rub-down from a sports masseur, my friend says—at least it was something like that. I've got to take it easy, take the long view, get to the end in one piece.

In corpore sana

I also sign up for Pilates. I've been told it's good for your core stability so should help with golf. Trouble is, the classes are all populated by ladies of a certain age and I don't fancy being the token man. Then one day I discover a police inspector—one of my playing partners—who's fitter and younger than me, goes on a Tuesday evening, so I sign up. After three weeks I'm totally into it. After four weeks, they cancel the class! I discover there is another on Wednesday lunchtimes, so I go through the ritual all over again. Thankfully there is also another bloke and this time he's *older* and fitter than me! Anyway, it soon becomes part of the routine and, believe it or not, I think it's beginning to help. I can now stand on my leg without falling over and a few times I've actually hit a golf ball without spinning off into space to the left. It's called "weight-shift" apparently. I also try the gym and toddle down with my wife one day, following her round the machines manfully increasing the resistance by about one notch each time. But I'm not really a gym animal. I really do prefer the great outdoors, so it's get on your bike and just get going; that's all I really need, not some sort of Popeye biceps. Anyway the pro says lower body strength is very important and it's really all about timing, not raw power.

It's going to take a lot of balls

Just how many balls am I going to get through playing unfamiliar courses for a month? Someone suggests I run a sweepstake on that; I write off to a couple of major ball manufacturers asking for sponsorship. Then there is all the other stuff I am going to need: are my clubs good enough? I really need a new bag, and a rain-suit. Will my GPS have all the courses loaded? Can I wear shorts at Walton Heath? Do I need tour kit with logoed shirts etc? Actually, it is a good time to go through my stuff and do a bit of a spring-clean so the gear list gets considerably longer:

- Balls—try to get sponsored otherwise it'll be the cheapest best
- Clubs—they're basically good but I need to learn to use that 4-wood
- Bag—new one needed, and I find a personalised one on the internet (£40)
- Shoes—2 new pairs should be enough (£70 in a sale)
- Gloves—1 a week, but do I need right-handed ones as well (£15)
- Wetsuit—I buy a top for £50 at *Golf Live* and get a free one worth £130 (??)
- GPS—I break out and get a fancy new one that's basically a watch too (£150)
- Trolley—I upgrade my somewhat rickety but working electric model (£260)
- Shirts—I'm going to have to get a set with logos made up (£100?) which reminds me . . .
- Washing—I'm going to have to do this regularly, which means . . .
- Travelling—I'm going to have to get back home every night, which means . . .
- The M25—is going to have to be my friend, or else . . .
- Accommodation—I'm going to have to find somewhere to stay every night!

Decisions, decisions, decisions. This thing has a life of its own now, but it doesn't half need feeding.

Er, is this actually legal?

Panic

So, let's see then, it's May. I've 3 months to go. I have 31 days of golf, 3 spaces available each day, that's 93 places to fill. Four days have filled up already—my golfing mates have snapped up some of the top venues—and I have at least one person for company on 13 other days. That leaves 14 days treading the fairways alone. 33% of places sold. I really do need to get the games up on that website.

Meanwhile Ian, ever the marketing man, is on about Press releases, media contacts, interviews etc. Big names are thrown around, but what if there's nothing to sell, just me and my golf buggy? And how am I going to raise that £3,000? Oh, it's £5,000 now, is it? Well, it's a round figure and if you sell all the golf spots you'll have no problem. I admire the optimism, but we need to sort out the details.

We meet up at Nell's Café for breakfast—it's right by the motorway, so creates the right mood—then on to the nearby golf club to get out the laptop, look at the website, see how it all works, plan our strategy etc. It's a lovely sunny day but we're not there to play golf, unfortunately. Just as well, we discover, as Ian has got cargo shorts on and they're a complete no-no! Oh dear, well at least we've only come for a meeting; we just need to get wi-fi. Can we get a coffee in the clubhouse? Er, no, did I not mention the cargo shorts? Ah, I've got some others in the car, I'll go and change, says Ian. Ah, yes, but then there are the trainers. Oh dear again. Well I have got my golf shoes, I could . . . no, not in the clubhouse, I'm afraid. Could we go on the terrace? Ah, but then you wouldn't have wi-fi . . .

Ian mumbles "this is what puts me off golf clubs"; I try to maintain my composure. The pro starts taking the spikes out of a pair of golf shoes, so they look like ordinary black shoes; Ian'll have to buy some white socks. I think that's not going to be a good look. He suggests putting on his overtrousers; no I don't think so; no outdoor clothing allowed. This is all going hopelessly pear-shaped. In the end we see the secretary, make a bit of a joke about it, get special dispensation and find a table in the corner which Ian can sit behind and not be seen. I'll go to the bar for the coffees. We are in the world of the members' club: we have to play by the rules. Pity we didn't know them before we came in.

The next hour is spent discussing the sociology of golf clubs, who they are for, what they do to attract visitors, whether they actually want to do that, whether they are really social clubs where you happen to be able to play golf and whether I'm going to get chucked out of half the clubs on the circuit for the wrong length of socks. Eventually, we get the website up and start discussing strategy. Two hours later, it's all sorted, the games will be posted, the branding agreed, the press releases sent out and we'll sit back and wait for the responses. Needless to say we don't stay for lunch, but a breakfast at Nell's café is good for the day so at least all is well on that front.

May 24th the first game goes on the site and the first taker bites. May 31st all 31 games are up there and we've doubled the capacity of The Social Golfer games pages. I check my spreadsheet and I'm still only 38% full and playing solo for 12 days. Still 2 months to go, though, no need to panic yet.

Throughout June and July, the media onslaught continues. The Downs Mail does a feature, Cancer Research UK get in touch for an interview, stuff goes out to golfing mags, BBC, ITV. We contact Chris Evans but he's on holiday. I go to Radio Kent. We start getting a mention here and there. I pick up free golf mags and see myself in there. The stakes are getting higher here. I wonder how we're doing on the take-up front. Mid June: 42% full, 12 days solo; end June: 54% full, 10 solo. At this rate I'm going to have a lonely August and not make a lot of money for cancer research. I set up a sweepstake on the number of shots I'll take as an additional way of raising funds. I get polo shirts printed with the Golf Against Cancer logo. I make up a couple of big sweetie jars to leave at the bar to collect money. I take back my cargo shorts to Marks and Spencers and change them for ordinary ones. I get a pack of blister plasters. I keep up the pilates. I keep off the fried breakfast.

Then we have The Open, Sandwich. That's a golf tournament, by the way, not something with tuna mayo. I go on the Friday and see the pictures of Seve all over Royal St George's. Anyway, it's a triumph for a Northern Irishman: not Rory McIlroy, the boy wonder from Hollywood, but Darren Clarke, who's nearly as old as me and was born only 10 miles away in Co Tyrone. A five on the last seals it for him. I get the bragging rights since I parred it on my last visit. Still he has played superbly and is now a national treasure. And of course he lost his wife Heather to cancer 6 weeks before the Ryder Cup in 2006. Ian does a new press release:

Ulsterman targets next Major . . .

Golf Against Cancer—A month of Madness on the M25!

Hot on the heels of Darren Clarke and Rory McIlroy, fellow Northern Irishman Trevor Sandford will be playing his way round the infamous London ring road this August, one junction a day (there are 31!), one course a day, raising funds for Cancer Research UK. We all know this is a great cause but with the recent loss of Seve Ballesteros it is even more relevant for golfers!

I pick up *English Club Golfer* to read "English club golfer Trevor Sandford . . ."; the *Kent Messenger* has "Trevor, from Bearsted,

Kent . . .".; now when it suits the media, I'm an Ulsterman. For once, though, it is fashionable to be from Northern Ireland and even cooler to be a golfer. Who cares, if it brings in more interest in the Month of Madness? I have a Welsh first name too, if that's any good to you.

Mid July, then. Two weeks to go and it's 62% full and 9 days solo. What's wrong with those 9 clubs I wonder? Why does no-one want to play there? Are they too expensive? No, actually most of them are the cheaper ones; the posh venues went first mainly. Some people cancel as they got their dates wrong. I get daily alerts from The Social Golfer announcing games the next day and I wonder if anyone plans ahead any more. Ian tells me not to worry, they will all fill up "nearer the time". I say it *is* nearer the time. My ever supportive wife emails her address book with the touching tale of Trevor no-mates and a few people come back in sympathy. I'm going away for a week immediately before the tour. I check the stats: 72% sold: 20 days full, 6 solo. Oh give me Darren Clarke's patience . . .

One of my other interests is choral singing. OK you can stop reading now. Well anyway I am off to Winchester for a week to sing in the Cathedral—all good traditional stuff, evensong and the like. I've 7 days to go before the month of golf and I have the audacity to take the week off to sing! Fortunately my marketing manager keeps me updated on the mobile and I nip out to the cloisters to do an interview for the Belfast Telegraph, English music and Irish golf taking turns for attention. I sheepishly tell my fellow choristers I am in the Sunday Mirror at the weekend—I am sure they are all Telegraph readers. One of them enters the sweepstake and goes for 2789 shots, but then he's not a golfer so what would he know? I kid myself that singing is actually helping my breathing and a week off the course will stop me getting golfed out.

I come back home the night before the tour. Suddenly there seems so much to do, but I start tomorrow: I read it in the paper so it must

TREVOR SANDFORD

be happening. I still have places to fill, I still have a few days when I'll be playing alone, but people say no, don't worry, we won't let that happen, so I'll see who my real friends are. I put away the suit, get out the shorts, pack up my bags and I'm ready to go. What awaits me on this month of madness only time will tell.

My bags are packed, I'm ready to go.

THE GAC TOUR:

A Month of Madness on the M25

Phew, what a scorcher!

Day 1: *Played Mid-Kent Golf Club, Gravesend, Kent with Ian M, John A & Chris E. Weather sunny, & hot (28˚C); scored 92 (27 points); walked 5.6 miles, lost 1 ball. A well-maintained members' club*

Every golf day begins with an obligatory coffee and bacon roll. These are actually separate items, but roll off the tongue together so well they must have been made for each other. Why bacon, I do not know, but one of these every day won't do a lot for my cholesterol level. Still, today is special and we'll have to start off in style. Unfortunately the club bar doesn't open until 11—there's an opportunity missed—so we're off to Nell's Diner, *"Where the Rich and Famous eat"* on the A2.

Nell's has a rich and famous history and though today I suspect few people feel the need to stop off here *en route* to the channel ferries, it still has a fair trade and offers a range of culinary delights. I go for the *Standard* option which features sausage, fried eggs (2), bacon (2), beans, fried bread and tomato at £5.80. For an extra 60p I could have had the *Whopper* with added mushrooms and bubble and squeak. Curiously, though, the *Light* option leaves out the sausage, beans and fried bread but still costs the same. With little economic incentive, perhaps it is no surprise that Kent sits high in the obesity ratings. Anyway, today I'll walk it all off and tomorrow I'll have slow-release complex carbohydrates, really I will.

I breakfasted with Ian, marketing manager and tour promoter. Never without his camera, he caught my wistful gaze at the passing traffic wondering what I'd let myself in for. Actually we've cheated today, I say, we won't actually touch the M25. Strictly speaking I should have gone up to the motorway and then turned off again, but we approach this one from the Kent side so there's no need. Anyway there is the peculiarity of there being two junctions—1a and 1b. You don't really notice this as you speed away from the Dartford toll-booths, but actually junction 1a is on the A284, so we can leave it out with a clear conscience; 31 junctions in 31 days and this is Day 1.

Ian had reserved a couple of places for media people, journalists etc. I won't say how I refer to them but I appreciate the opportunity to raise the profile of the tour by having it promoted from within, as it were. Anyway, at the weekend various half promises and maybes had turned to nought and I'd phoned him to release the slots to see if anyone else actually wanted to play. Within the day we had a couple of sign-ups: John, who is doing a week in Essex at the end of the month and Chris, who was due to play elsewhere today but pulled out to join us here. A great start to the month, with a full team of four.

Full of breakfast and trepidation in equal measure, we hoof it round the corner to the golf club. Ian has remembered not to wear cargo shorts so we should gain entry OK. When we do, we find a large blackboard proclaiming:

> MONDAY 1ST AUGUST
> 1ST TEE CLOSED 10.50-11.10
> 1X4 BALL FOR CHARITY
> "A MONTH OF GOLF"
> CANCER RESEARCH

Hey, we're expected, warmly welcomed in fact. Mark the pro is away but Dan sorts everything out for us and shortly the first tee is set up like a proper tournament with Cancer Research UK and The Social Golfer banners all in place and ready to go. We putt and warm up as the club veterans go out in their fourballs ahead of us in their monthly medal. Numerous group photos are taken and finally the Month of Golf actually gets under way with a 145 yard uphill par 3. I risk a 9-iron as the wind's behind and make the green, only to follow with a 3-putt, the ups and downs of a month of madness in evidence already. Only 557 holes to go, says Ian, ever encouraging and supportive . . .

When the dust settles a bit, I don't actually play too badly, making a birdie on the par-5 3rd but following immediately with a double-bogey on the next. The next birdie on 11 is followed by a triple bogey on the 12th. Why is golf so maddening? I could blame the wind, I suppose, or even the hot weather. In August 2003, Gravesend broke all records, coming in at above 38°C. Today, a good 10 degrees lower and with a decent breeze, it was actually a pleasure to be out there playing golf. The course was lovely, well manicured and quite lush despite the lack of rain. The greens were quick and true, with few excuses for human error.

We arrive at the last and I rip one off the tee, a full 310 yards down the fairway. That'll impress the vets as they sip their shandy on the terrace, someone mutters and yes, there they are, finished their game and waiting for the M25 man to come in, or so it appears. All eyes on my simple 100-yarder home, I fluff it short, then find a bunker, scramble out and, two putts later, finish with some relief for a 6. One moment you are hitting like Rory McIlroy, the next like a 30-handicapper. Oh well, there is always tomorrow. I'm done and in with a 92, 10 over my handicap, and ready for a drink.

I wonder how bad my golf is going to get over this month, but then that's not really the point of it. If I'd wanted to improve, I'd have booked a series of lessons. This is about raising money. That message has got over to one or two of the vets on the terrace and they offer some cash to help me along. The forty quid in the cookie-jar at the bar adds to the

£90 my partners have paid to play golf, making £130 raised for cancer research. 31 times that would be . . . er, now where's my calculator?

Back home after a bath and a glass of wine, I have cooled down enough to feel nearly normal, washed out the team shirts, updated the spreadsheet with today's stats, done a course review on The Social Golfer website and compiled episode 1 of the tour blog. Who knows whether anyone will look at any of it, but we are away now and I realise that this is going to be more or less a full-time job. When am I going to get time to eat? Fortunately tonight my daughter is "practising her cooking for university" and treats us to a wonderful chicken satay. Mmm . . . In my day the best you got was baked beans. But we had them at Nell's diner, which was just as well, as I realise I've completely missed lunch.

I have, however, got through several litres of water. The golf wasn't always too hot but if the weather stays like this I'm going to be exhausted. That memorable tabloid headline from 1976 offers itself to encapsulate the day and I take it up. *Phew, what a scorcher* announces Day 1 of the tour to my website readers. This weather can't last, so they need to get out now and join me. Only 30 more days (and 540 holes) to go.

One down, 30 to go.

Del-boy makes a difference

Day2: *Played Birchwood Park Golf Centre with Kamal L & Arthur C. Hot, sunny (28°C). Scored 82 (37 points); walked 6.8 miles, lost 1 ball. A popular pay&play venue*

So what am I doing at a pay-and-play, then? Isn't there a nice members' club somewhere in Dartford? Actually there is, *and* it's nearer Junction 2; it's just that not everything works out the way you plan it. I remember the phone call now. I'd sent the email and had tried several times to follow up, leaving messages, returning calls without success etc. When I did get through, I could hear they were busy and the person in the office, no doubt covering the receiver to no effect, was saying "I've got that Golf Against Cancer bloke again . . . no, we don't want anything today, tell him" and I'm thinking could I just explain what I'm after, I'm not trying to sell you something, but they were just up to their eyes and life was too short to annoy them anymore, so it was time to move on.

Actually there's a 9-hole course nearer junction 2 than either of them, but I've played at Birchwood before, it's not a bad course and I got a good reception when I called to ask for a tee-time so in the diary it went. It's Arthur's local course so I know he'll play and my musician friend Dave lives nearby: he's just getting into golf, so he'll give it a go too. Nearer the time Alan from The Social Golfer (TSG) books the fourth slot. Somehow, though, it's not a lucky venue for bookings. I'm doing a gig with Dave a couple of weeks before; he does an impressive harmonica solo, sits down and then collapses on the floor. Seems fine and chirpy when the ambulance comes and we finish the concert without him, but it transpires he's had an aortic aneurism and is lucky to be alive. Several weeks later when I see him at the next rehearsal, I promise to take him out in a couple of months when he's fully recovered—he's paid in advance so I owe it to him and am thankful he'll actually be able to take me up on it.

Kamal takes the spare place, so we're up to four again. Then Alan has to pull out due to a family emergency just the day before. He's paid too, so I suggest he books in for another day and we'll go ahead with three. Talking of which, my mother always said bad things happen in threes, so I'm just waiting to see what else is going to go wrong today. I don't have to wait too long. I set up my electric trolley in the car park and find it's completely dead. Hang on, folks, this is a *new* trolley, used about 5 times, bought specially for the tour, what kind of luck is this? I'm already stressed up with setting up everything on my own and we tee off in about ten minutes. The helpful guy in the pro-shop says no problem, mate, have a pull-trolley on the house and my blood pressure begins to settle again.

Actually, they are all very helpful here. As indeed they have been most places. Once they log who you are in the pro-shop and they know what you are doing, they are keen to help out. "It's booked with Nicola (or whoever)" is the usual kind of password. And there is a lot to sort out when you arrive at the club. Book in, make yourself known, see the secretary/manager or whoever gave you the tee-time (if they're about), ask if you can put up a couple of banners on the first tee/18th green, ask if you can leave a charity collecting jar at the bar, see the bar manager, tell them what you're doing and encourage them to draw attention to the collection etc etc. Meanwhile your playing partners are arriving/have arrived, made themselves known (if they're not already friends, that is) and they want to know what's happening too. There's always a photocall on the first tee, where you can usually persuade someone else to do a group shot with the Cancer Research UK banner in evidence and then other opportunities to take photos during the round. Yesterday Ian did all this whilst I just played golf; today it's down to me.

And then I met my saviour for the day. Del was at the starter's hut pushing the groups out on time when I arrived with the banners. The ground was hard and unyielding; it was a job to make any dent in it. Off he went and got some tools, watered the parched earth to soften it up, hammered in the posts, all no trouble. Drove me to the 18th green, picked the best spot where it'd be seen from far away and had a go at setting up my second banner there. Now this was a bit of a homemade version, mounted on a couple of my wife's gardening canes. Hmmm, not very strong he thought. It'll be broken by the end of the day, I agreed. Anyway, we have to get off now, so thanks for being such a great help. Wish I could have done more, he says, if only I'd known you were coming, I could have got a few more people together to support you. I only do 2 charities—Help the Heroes and Cancer Research. Turns out his son has been diagnosed with lung cancer at 47. Not even a smoker I think but now a victim. Early days but he's having treatment. No wonder he responded to the Cancer Research logo—it struck to the heart of his nearest and dearest, and he gave back generously.

Inspired by Del's kindness—or perhaps eager to impress the bunch of teenage boys waiting to follow us—I spank my first drive 290 yards down the fairway and we're away. This augurs well for a good round and I realise why. Though only a few miles away from yesterday's venue, this is a more exposed site on sandy soil and it's practically bare after so little rain. The ball runs for miles, which makes all our drives look impressive. Even more so those of the teenagers behind who *are* actually hitting the ball like Rory McIlroy, or at least trying to. This gets to Arthur on the second hole. We've spent a while looking for my ball and the boys are getting impatient. Arthur's setting up to go for the green and a ball comes bouncing by off the tee. Not good. Are we going to have a fight here, I wonder? No, it's golf and we're all polite and so on, but it's a bit rude at least, not to say dangerous, as they come up behind and a few words are exchanged.

Having nearly lost my ball, I make a birdie to go with a couple of pars and I start working on calming Arthur down. He finds his game and helps us around this varied track, picking the best line off each tee and so on. I don't find too many fairways off the tee, but a 5-iron from the fairway bunker on the last flies all of 200 yards setting up a birdie putt. I go out in 42 and back in 40-10 shots better than yesterday: a couple of birdies, lots of pars and nothing disastrous, one under my handicap overall. Not a bad day at the office. Coming in off the 18th, I see the charity banner still standing and notice that someone has found a metal rod and taped it on to hold the thing up against the wind—nice one.

In the bar, a lot quieter now than it was first thing, we have a drink and Arthur's wife Carole comes down to join us. Apparently she takes her mum here every week for lunch—it's the best food in the area. I am tempted but have promised my daughter I'll have room for her pasta carbonara tonight. Still, I'll have to sort out the lunch thing—you can only have a certain number of bananas. I pick up the charity jars as I get ready to go. There's a total of £7.43: doesn't really match the £40 I got yesterday, but then why would it? Yesterday we followed the Veterans' Medal—average age 70. Today it was more like 17, with lads on their school holidays spending their pocket money on a day out on the course. Not a *silver pound* in sight. They can't hit a golf ball as far but maybe those 70 year olds have got something over the teenagers after all . . .

I'm not completely done yet as I go to collect the banners from the course and find they've disappeared. Oh no, they haven't been nicked, have they—or chucked away? They have to do me another 29 days. I find they've been left back in the pro-shop for me, metal supports and all. I'm on my way out to the car park, it's going home time now and who should I see in a buggy waiting to go but my friend Del-boy from this morning. I pop over to thank him, saying the metal posts are ingenious, well done. Tell you what, says he, you can have 'em and I go away with a banner that's likely to last me a month rather than a couple of days and a greater appreciation of the contribution of the "little people" in life, the people who do small things that make a big difference. Thanks, Del.

It's only when I get back to the car I remember about the trolley so tonight, after the carbonara, out comes the spanner and the back yard becomes a trolley repair shop. After a short investigation, it all points to the battery. Surely I haven't forgotten to charge it, but it seems completely dead. Further stripping down reveals a weakness in the connector where a wire has simply come out of a socket. Ideally it should be soldered but pliers and a screwdriver do the job and it's back on charge ready for the morning. Phew, I wasn't looking forward to pulling a trolley around for a month; you do rely on these things, don't you?

Now it's wash the hands and get online to do my homework for the day: stats, review, blog, admin, money etc. It won't take me too long to count the money tonight, but somehow I am a whole lot richer than when I started and that's due to the generosity of human nature I have discovered when I was least expecting it.

Penal rough awaits the rich and famous

Day 3: London Golf Club with Steve H, Mervyn & John W. Sunny, hot (30 °C), windy. Shot 97 (25 pts); walked 7.9 miles lost 3 balls. A classy, challenging Tour venue

OK perhaps we have stretched a tad over 5 miles from junction 3 here—in fact Birchwood yesterday was closer—but you can't go past a course which has hosted the European Open without giving it a try. Anyway, it's right next to the M20, so preserves its motorway credentials. Pity we won't actually be able to play the Jack Nicklaus designed Heritage course—it's reserved for members and, of course, tour events. However, I've played the International before and it's a good test, well worth the £100 I'm asking my playing partners to fork out today and the venue itself is just classy. I did a photo-shoot here for the Sunday Mirror article a couple of weeks ago so I know my way around.

Mervyn lives round the corner and has offered to drive me today. He tried to pop in to the London Club before, just to have a mosey around but met a polite refusal at the gate. Sorry, you do need to have business here it seems. Well today I did and as we pull up and lower the window the security guard welcomes me by name and wishes me a good day on the course. Nice. The 5* treatment continues as you drop off your bags at the door; they'll be waiting for you on the trolley/buggy or whatever later. Park up and go for a coffee, we've plenty of time in hand. I do the usual stuff in the pro-shop. Dan is away today but they're expecting me and yes of course you can put those banners up—just leave them with us and we'll see to it, Sir.

Oh and then the first bit of bad news. We're terribly sorry but the International course is closed for maintenance, we've put you on the Heritage instead, hope that's OK. Well we are obviously gutted to have to play on the same turf where I last witnessed the boy wonder tackle the European Open, but, hey, we'll get over it. Oh and do have a strokesaver with our compliments . . .

I head over to the bar to wait for the others and see someone I recognise. It's Steve Backley OBE, local lad, Olympic silver medallist and former javelin world record holder, looking fit as ever in his golf shorts. He's the Club President and just in from an early round on the course. Well clearly I need to thank him for the club's generosity today, so I introduce myself and we get talking about what I'm here today to do. The course is playing great, he says, but the rough is really penal, you don't want to go in there. What do you play off? Twelve? Well, 95 would be a good score. Now there's my challenge for the day.

Time to reveal my secret to Steve, from my golfing society, who's playing today with Mervyn and me. Who's the fourth, he asked in an email? I said all will be revealed and he said are we talking celeb and I said wait and see. Well in the great tour promotion phase of June/July, Ian handled the national and golfing press and I said I'd cover local contacts so I got a column in the Kent Messenger a couple of weeks before. I also rung the BBC. Well Chris Evans was on his hols but I knew that John Warnett, the early morning show presenter on Radio Kent, was a keen golfer so I sent him all the info. I called every day when I was in Winchester to catch him before he left the office (at 9.10 am!) and eventually got him, so yes of course he'd be delighted to come, do an interview for the show and then play golf.

So we're sitting chatting to Steve Backley like we are old mates and Steve (H) is thinking, crikey Trev, how did you get hold of him, then, when in walks Warnett, mike in hand, hot from his morning show. Of course he chats away with Steve B for ages as they'd just done an interview yesterday about the Olympics or something and it's all jolly banter until the club president has to go and we are left with our fourball and John says shall we get on with the interview then? Now Steve (H) is well confused. Who are we actually playing with, Trevor? Well there's you, me, Mervyn and . . .

I've done interviews with John before several times when I was in local government in Kent. It was normally either good news (we are opening a new skills centre . . .) or bad news (School X has just been failed by Ofsted), but today I do not have to carry the burden of local politics, I can just be myself and enthuse about the Month of Golf. John tees me up and I drive the message home for cancer research etc. Hopefully that'll raise the profile, maybe get a few more sign-ups and generate some more cash for the cause. I ask him for the contacts for his opposite numbers in Surrey, Hertfordshire etc so they can track me on my way round. No problem. Now let's play golf.

Last time I was here it was for *Golf Live* and it was buzzing; today there's hardly anyone about, so we have plenty of time for first-tee photos, with the Cancer Research UK banner all set up waiting for us, on its shiny new metal stakes. Formalities over, we're reaching for the driver when along comes the starter, a charming Irishman. Have you played here before? No. Well, the rough is really penal, let me warn you. Otherwise, gave a great day. Guess what happens next? We all four step up and all find the rough. Even my provisional is well off line. This is going to be a tough round.

Stupid, really, because the fairway is not particularly narrow. It's just the fear factor which has been instilled in you by all these warnings. After a couple of holes, there's an easy par 3 which restores our confidence and we start to play golf. I've taken three to reach the spot where Rory hit his drive the day I watched him here and took a sand wedge to the par-5 5th green. I take an 8-iron and just find the water, making a 7. This course is not designed for mere mortals. Actually the par 5s are reachable in 2 from the forward tees, but the greens are so well protected you're dead if you miss; that's the difference between the pros and us hackers. Still, Mervyn, occasional golfer allegedly off 24, is now getting serious backspin with his 9 iron and he and Steve have me and John 4 down by the 13th. It's such a pretty hole, I've been concentrating on taking photos and not playing golf and fire my 6-iron into deep rough; should have taken a seven. I'll know for again.

| At least I'm a leftie | Unfortunately I'm not |

You know you've been out here when you get to the last. It's hilltop windy and you've had to focus on every shot to avoid rough, water, bunkers etc. You stand on the last looking at a fairway with a big lake to the left and somehow your assessment of your abilities completely deserts you. At the *Golf Live* show, I saw World Long Drive Champion, Joe Miller clear the pond with a 450-yard drive and then do it again—

with a putter! Now it's my turn. The 4-wood for safety goes straight in, so I take a drop and finish off 2 short of my target score of 95. Only 2 pars and 2 disastrous par-3s; otherwise not too bad on a course set up for professionals: harder than Royal St George's IMHO.

Two drinks on the terrace later and two guys roll up on the 18th in a buggy. Backley and his mate finish their third round of the day. I tell him I made 97; he smiles. I've had a terrific day: burned by the sun, blown by the wind and beaten by the course, but enjoyed every minute of it. He gets to come here every day and it counts as work! I suspect he knows every corner of the course pretty well, though, playing off 6, I doubt he knows the rough as well as we do.

Swingin' in the rain

Day 4: *Broke Hill with Chris S. Rain: heavy and prolonged. Shot 87 (35pts); walked 6 miles, lost 1 ball. Too wet to play golf*

It had to happen—it's the British summer. After three days of heat, the weather broke so today's destination was aptly named. I'd played the neighbouring pay&play course before and thought that this, a members' club under the same management, would offer a good alternative. I'd even seen games advertised there on TSG, so it must be OK. However I started the month with nobody booked in until, just a couple of days before, Chris signed up, thus saving me trudging round on my own. However, I'm not sure he looked at the weather forecast.

There was a lot to look forward to today. I'd had an email from the club saying that a film crew would be there to make some sort of documentary. No, it wasn't Sky Sports, unfortunately, but the Orpington and District Film and Video Society, no less. Next stop Hollywood. They specialise in comedy and drama, apparently. Well I can provide both of those, but today the big feature is a newsreel of "interesting events in Orpington during 2011" in which I am scheduled to appear alongside Kate Middleton opening a school and stuff like that. Also, Gary from the club had offered a free buggy. Normally, I'd have said no, but looking at the weather and seeing there were just the two of us, my scruples soon evaporated.

Hmm, not sure we are letting buggies out today, said the pessimist in the pro-shop. Well, obviously if they're not allowed, fine, but if they are I'll definitely be using one! Strokesaver? That'll be £3.50. Why did I suddenly think that was mean? After all, they'd just given me a buggy costing £25, so really I was happy to pay for the course planner. Yes of course I could put the banners up, but it would be up to me to do it. Maybe it was just the contrast from yesterday, where all of this was taken off my hands. I was just getting spoiled and a bit carried away by being a star of the silver screen.

Mike Turner arrives with his wife, carting camera gear—it's the film crew. The first part is fine as he does an interview indoors all about the project and the girls at the bar give us all a free coffee. Then we have to go outside. By this time Chris has arrived. We're both togged out in full rainwear as it's pretty much set in now, but head off to the first tee for the obligatory photos, today of the moving picture variety. Best swing needed here, so I'll take a little rescue club. Not bad but my second finds the greenside bunker and now I have a camera staring at me and it's chucking it down. I get out to about 20 feet and then, with a howling gale, driving rain and people waiting on the fairway wondering what on earth we are up to, I can the putt on the first take. Thank goodness, because I don't think Tony is staying for any more. I think I've got enough here, he says, so I run him back to the first tee, let the next group through and brace myself for a soggy day at the office.

As we splash along the fairway through casual water, I give Chris the option of calling it a day now but he's made of sterner stuff and anyway, his wife's dropped him off and gone to work so he's stuck here with me whatever. We can't putt on any of the greens as they are basically flooded by now, so anything close is a gimme, but we manage to keep our spirits up with "how mad are we?" kind of banter and even get a bit of a match on until I lose a ball on the 9th, taking a dreadful 9 shots. We're now back at the clubhouse; temptation mounts and the inevitable happens: Chris calls it a day and phones the wife for a pick-up. I carry on manfully, wondering if there is anyone else left out on the course. Actually Chris has been a bit of a hero just playing the front 9. No-one in their right mind would choose to play golf today. I just didn't have the choice and of course left my right mind a very long time ago.

Playing golf solo is a curious pastime. You do get round quicker, as long as people let you through, but it somehow takes a lot of the point out of it. You'd get more practice on the range and a better walk somewhere else. Also there's no-one to help you find your ball. The temptation to take easy gimmes, numerous mulligans or just give up entirely is always there. Normally I play two balls and score one of them, playing against the other. Today, however, I'd just like to get home to a warm bath; yesterday's heat is a distant memory.

I discover there is practically no-one still out, so I park up under a tree and have a three-course lunch: pork pie, banana and a cereal bar, washed down with a little Chateau d'Eau—excellent, a fine vintage. The rain abates a little and the golf actually improves—5 pars on the back 9. I'm getting plenty of practice dobbing a little rescue club off every tee so I won't lose sight of the ball in the low cloud. It looked a nice course; I couldn't really tell, I was too busy wiping my glasses to see much; maybe I'll come back here and play this on a normal day. However, disaster is never far away and on the 16th the ball goes 230 yards and the club goes 40. Get a grip, Trev, literally. Just get in and get home.

Eventually I made the clubhouse and discovered why they were prepared to give me that rain suit free with a £50 top. I was soaked to the skin. I've only been this wet once before. It was during the Captain's Cup at my home club when they abandoned after 9 holes. I was keen to play on as I had 19 points and was playing well. So was Richard, who had 18. Trouble was, it had been a 2-tee start so I'd played the front 9 and he'd played the back, so we couldn't have carried on together even if we'd wanted to. Today I had no such dilemmas. With the full weight of Golf Against Cancer on my shoulders, I'd carried on and, in a curious way, actually enjoyed it. I've still got 3 days ahead with nobody booked, and they can't be as bad as this. All good character-building stuff, I thought.

Typical August weather

Deciding there was no point in having a shower as I'd nothing dry to change into, I collected up my stuff to go. Clearly it wasn't a good day for the sweetie jar. I saw Gary and thanked him for the buggy—it was a life-saver; I hope I haven't churned up the course too much. I paddled to the car and drove home, longing to get back and into the jacuzzi. Then, as I turned off the motorway and up into my front drive, just for fun, the sun came out. Four down, 27 to go, but I think I must be over the worst of it already.

Lexus for Sale, SatNav extra

Day 5: Wildernesse Club with Jed, Paul C & Gary. Sunny, warm. Shot 90 (33pts); walked 7.8 miles, lost 1 ball. Lovely course for a two-ball

It's a costly mistake: you only make it once. I'd used Junction 5 many times when coming from the West Country to visit my sister in Hastings but it was only after I moved to Kent that I discovered its shortcomings. Racing along the M26, late as usual, for a meeting in Tunbridge Wells, I looked for the A21 turn-off and it never came. Twenty-two miles later, having no doubt broken the speed limit by an even greater margin, I was heading south, having gone halfway into Surrey and back. Why they never made a turn-off here I do not know. Even my mate Andy, who knows everything about the M25, doesn't know. I've looked on the satellite map and seen the field where it could have been; I've looked at the nice house with the tennis court nearby and wondered who lived there when the motorway was built and whether they had any influence. Why did the burghers of Sevenoaks not want people turning left at this particular junction? It means that if you *do* want to get there from the M26, you have to turn off *miles* earlier and go through lots of villages: Platt, Borough Green, Seal etc

Yes, junction 5 is one of the five "limited access" junctions on the M25. (For the geeks, the others are 1b, 19, 21 and 31. 1a as we know is not a motorway junction. Did you get that earlier? There'll be a test afterwards, you know.) It's mentioned daily on the Radio Kent traffic news; it's always a bottleneck; Andy and I argue over which lane is the quicker and you think of avoiding it if you can. So to turn off here you have to go up to junction 3 and down again. Well, as I've said, I'm not being a purist, so today I toddle off through the villages along the A25, leaving loads of time, just in case junction 5 is playing up and everybody else chooses to do the same. I know where I'm going today; I've had a vague look at the map just to check so I don't need the SatNav. Passing through Seal, I see a sign pointing left to "Golf Club" and wonder why I hadn't noticed a course there on my Google Maps planning trawl.

I did have a few other options in the area, even if you couldn't actually get off at junction 5 to get to any of them. However, Wildernesse looked like a good bet. A members' club dating from 1890, with tree-lined fairways, it was somewhere Jed had wanted to play for ages and it was his birthday so I'd booked him in and he was going to bring a couple of friends. It had even gone to the club committee for approval. It was definitely going to be a treat, and definitely *not* a cargo shorts day! Then with about 2 weeks to go, Jed pulled out as he had to work that morning, so I was left with a really nice venue and no-one to play with.

I generally try to avoid working on my birthday if I can manage it. Ask any of my previous bosses. Usually I take the day off rather than just slacking, but apparently Jed couldn't do that. It was a County Council meeting and he had to go. Pity. Then in a blinding flash of insight, I rung up one morning and asked if we could play in the afternoon. No problem, they said. Why hadn't I thought of that before? I'd just thought midweek 11 am, weekend 2pm and that was that. However, now, with a pm tee-time, Jed could go to his meeting and still join us and actually so could a couple of others. I wondered how many other games would have filled up faster if they'd been in the afternoon.

All this could be entirely theoretical, however, as I still haven't actually found it yet. I did think I knew where it was, but somehow it's not proving easy to locate. I stop and ask directions and find myself in a maze of private roads lined by enormous mansions until I come to a barrier across the road with a keypad entrance. Oh, no, I'm going to have to find my way all the way back. I get out to have a look, walk round to the front of the barrier and—hey, there's a notice saying "Key 9537 ENTER", so I do and the barrier lifts, allowing me in. Or is it out? I don't recall going in anywhere but you never know. It does strike me as odd that an exclusive estate of private residences tells the casual passer-by the entry code. Perhaps the residents had got forgetful, or maybe the inconvenience of getting out of the vehicle to read the sign is considered deterrent enough. Anyway, thankfully I've left plenty of time today and I get to the club well before my tee-off time.

No entry for Lexus drivers.

Nice wooded entrance . . . big car park . . . must have a healthy membership . . . and a wealthy one too judging by the number of *Lexus* RX460s around. I nearly got run over by one as it edged in to park— these hybrid engines are so quiet, you don't know they are around. My old IS200 is beginning to look decidedly scruffy alongside. Anyway, having got here at last, I'm really looking forward to the game. It takes a while to sort out the admin, see the secretary, visit the pro-shop, get the banners up and the charity jars out, work out which door needs a code, where you can go with golf shoes and whether they have free towels in the clubhouse. All that done, I get out and see my fourball have all found each other so, being their leader, I am obliged to follow and we head off for the first for a photo.

Hang on, now, what was the arrangement? Fourballs off the first tee before 1.15 and off the 10th after 1.15 was it? What time is it now? Ten past one and here comes a twoball. Better get off to the 10th then, so we go round the other side of the clubhouse and tee-up ready to go. Hang on again, this looks long for a par-3; it should be 177 yards—it looks over 300 . . . er, maybe this isn't the 10th . . . er, what's it say on the tee? . . . oh, it's the 14th! Then where's the 10th? . . . oh, there was a sign somewhere. I do wonder whether this club ever has visitors. Well we do find it, after what seems like a half-mile walk and I think what would have been wrong with starting on the 14th? Why is it that golfers have to work in nines all the time? Or if they do, why don't they put the 10th in a sensible place, e.g. near the clubhouse? And why do you start in a different place depending on how many of you there are—how is that going to work out? Oh the unfathomable mysteries of golf.

Paul and I take on Gary and Jed in a match. Paul starts with a par and I birdie the second, so we're motoring by the 13th, a short par-3, no more than a pitching wedge. A 2-ball has come up behind, so we let them play up after us and then go through. This gives me a larger audience for the nearest I have ever got to a hole-in-one in ten years of playing golf—a mere five inches away! I know it's just luck but, as Sir Nick Faldo said when he chipped in from a bunker, "That's what I was trying to do"! Playing off 13 now, on the 13th hole, I'm 13 centimetres out—how unlucky is that?

TREVOR SANDFORD

As near to a hole-in-one as I am likely to get.

I have peaked too early, though, and the round progresses with bogey golf, apart from an unfortunate 8 on the par-5 6th. The sun shines, the sky is blue, the woods bathed in dappled light and the course is great. Unfortunately they've only just done annual maintenance on the greens, so they are full of little holes and covered with sand. Normally a club will give you a discounted green fee in these circumstances, but since they've given me this for nothing I can't really complain. It hasn't spoiled the round and it gives me an excuse for missing putts. I get in with a 90, which, at 33 points, feels like a decent score.

During the round another couple of twoballs have come up behind and, playing a lot quicker than us, have been let through. The worst case was when we came off the 18th to go through to the 1st just as a group were going to start. We let them go ahead and whiled away the time with the first-tee photos we'd not taken before, our swings well warmed up from the previous 9 holes. In the end though, we took over

5 hours for our round. Was it all the waiting around as we let faster groups through out of courtesy? Hard to tell, but it did cut down our drinking time on the terrace on a beautiful evening as Jed had to get off to celebrate his birthday, if not his golf (we beat 'em big time).

At least all those two-balls would have got in before us and noticed the charity collecting jar strategically placed in the bar. I was hopeful of a few bob more here in affluent Sevenoaks today than I managed to pick up after my lonely trek in yesterday's rain. And sure enough, there was some in there, even if most of it was just loose change. Still, loose change to a Lexus driver is like the sound of their engine—a quiet rustle rather than a noisy rattle. Totting up at home it came to £49.05, the best day so far. With £50 each for the golf, we were up to the £200 mark for the day, so not bad, considering that a week ago, I was going to be playing round here on my own. Now I've just got to do that tomorrow—*and* tackle the M25 proper to boot.

I had time to get all my homework done tonight, as I got back in about half the time it had taken me to get there. Turning right out of the golf club exit instead of taking on the gated estate, I found myself a couple of hundred yards later in the village of Seal, looking at a little sign saying "Golf Club" pointing back where I'd come from. If only I'd had the sense to take this turn on my way in, I'd have missed all that faffing about getting through the barrier and a considerable detour. Maybe from tomorrow I stop trying to be a man, admit I don't know the way and put on the Sat Nav . Hmmm, the new IS250 has one fitted as standard; maybe I'll have another look at that *Lexus* brochure when I get a moment.

Wise Men come from the East

Day 6: North Downs Golf Club with Andy P & David H. Windy, cool, overcast. Shot 87 (32 pts); walked 5.9 miles, lost 4 balls. Short & sweet but a sting at the turn

Junction 6 today: no more faffing around on the M20, M26 or any of that. Today is the moment we've been waiting for: we leave Kent and hit the M25 proper. And guess what happens? It's closed. No, surely not, I cry in dismay. Yes it is, says my dear wife. OK, then it must be true. It's all over the internet, And the radio. And TV. Must have been a big one, says Andy. Probably a fuel load or something that takes ages to clear up, he says from bitter experience.

Hmm, 6 is obviously not my lucky number. It's been quite difficult fixing this up. It was last Christmas and I still hadn't got a venue for this date. It's the first Saturday of the tour and it's proved much harder to get a tee-time at the weekend. You can understand why. People generally work during the week and then Saturday and Sunday they go and play golf. It's quite normal for a club to have no guests until after noon at the weekend, if at all. So I recalled the telephone conversation with Andrew Tanner, Club Secretary at Tandridge:

Yes Trevor, happy to help you out. What about Thursday 4th?

Well, I was looking at Saturday 6th. Is that possible?

No, I'm afraid I can't do the Saturday at all. What about the following week—Tuesday 9th or Wednesday 10th anytime would be possible.

Ah, no, but I'll be at Junction 9 or 10 by then, you see. I'm making my way round the M25. You're near Junction 6, so it has to be Saturday 6th.

Well, that's a bit of a restriction, I'm afraid. Terribly sorry, but we've got nothing then; absolutely chock-a-block with members at the weekend. I think you'll probably find that elsewhere too.

And of course, I did. Same at Bletchingly, Westerham, anywhere I asked really. I did get one offer from a club I didn't fancy, and they were a bit far away anyway, so I was pleased in the end when North Downs came up trumps. Not a club I'd heard of before but looked nice on the website and friendly on the phone so in it went. Unfortunately, none of my golfing buddies had heard of it either and it lacked the draw of, say, Walton Heath, so it had sat unbooked for a long time: it looked like I was going to be playing there on my own. Then the day before, David signed up from TSG, rescuing me from solitude and, on top of that, Andy got back from his hols, gave me a call and said he'd be coming too—and he'd give me a lift. Now there's a pal when you need it.

Understandably, his wife also looks out for him so *both* of us were festooned with quotes from the travel websites such as "Avoid the area at all costs" etc etc. However, the ladies know by now that when there is a game of golf to be played, normal logic goes out the window, so, with mumbles of "we'll be fine", we set off, leaving plenty of time for the journey.

What I perhaps should have said is that the motorway was closed between junctions 7 and 8—in *both* directions. But since we were getting off at Junction 6, we reckoned there wouldn't be a problem, and so it transpired. In fact, such was the effectiveness of the multitude of warnings that anyone planning to use that bit of the motorway had stayed away entirely and we sailed through to Jn6 in record time, ignoring all the flashing lights and matrix boards. It did enable us to exchange some "interesting facts about the M25", of which more anon, discussing the new cats-eyes and commenting on the rutting from the super-sixes. Oh, didn't I say? Andy's an engineer who was in charge of maintenance of this stretch for years, so he does know a bit about it.

Getting there well in advance of our tee-time, we were given a warm welcome, a quick tour of the clubhouse and the invitation to go off whenever we were ready. In fact, a number of groups had started on the 8th (don't ask why . . .) so now would actually be a good time to go as the course was clear. Well that would have been fine for the two of us, but David was coming from somewhere else, so we'll be happy to wait. Let's go and do a bit of putting practice, shall we?

Now here's a unique feature of this particular club. The 18th green is enormous, but one end of it doubles up as the practice putting green for the course! So you're on there, finely honing your six-footers when somebody thins their lob wedge from forty feet and sends you running for cover? No, you just keep an eye out and step back for a moment as they play their shots in. Amazingly, it seems to work. At least I didn't notice anyone sporting an eye patch or on crutches, so I guess it must do.

After several coffees a message arrives that David is stuck on the motorway. Ah, where is he coming from? Junction 10. Oh dear, that could be a problem. Start without me, he says, so we wait for a bit, but eventually have to take to the turf as a 2-ball. Andy and I start a match and he pars the first four holes: I'm definitely going to be buying the drinks today. I'm just getting back in the game on the fifth when someone walks up saying "You must be Trevor". It's David; he's made it, through the highways and byways of Surrey, by all accounts, having taken two and a half hours to travel about 15 miles. "Well, you'll be ready for a game of golf, then" is my sensitive cheery reply. He doesn't know why I am so pleased, but he has rescued me from a beating at the hands of my regular golf partner!

It's a nice course, short and sweet, so the rescue club/lob wedge formula works pretty well, until we come to the 10th, which is Stroke Index 1, the hardest hole on the course. I've already lost 2 balls in the brambles on the 9th, so I'm cautious about the tee-shot as there's Out of Bounds all down the left. It turns out fine but now for the second there's OB all down the *right* and it's a long way uphill. After clouting 2 balls over the hedge, I take a triple bogey and move on. Four balls lost in 2 holes! I'm going to have to buy more at this rate. Why does a course seduce you for the front nine and then knife you in the back over a couple of holes? In the end, I come away with an 87, eighteen over par, bogey golf, which may be about standard for a player of my ability on unfamiliar terrain. We get in as the rain begins, just, and David stays for a drink before he tackles the return journey.

At the bar I see they have their own Cancer Research collecting jars. It's the Lady Captain's charity apparently and they're very interested in what I'm doing for it. Tell you what, mate, leave the jar with us till tomorrow and we'll make sure there's a bit more in it, can you? OK, why not? I'm not too far down the road and I can always nip back and pick it up; I've got two after all.

I suppose we ought to be getting on, now. Our 2.15 start means it's now about 7 o'clock. The motorway is still shut and David wonders when he will see home. I thank him profusely for making the effort for just 13 holes of golf and offer him his money back, but it's for charity and he's happy to let it go. He's paid a far greater price in wrestling with the traffic on the way and he's going to have to do it again to get home. For us, it'll be easy peasy because nobody will be coming our way.

Later on the BBC news website, I learn that Transport Minister Norman Baker is to look into why it took more than 24 hours to reopen the M25 after a crash which left three people badly hurt. Mr Baker said the Department of Transport (DoT) would be looking into the incident "in some detail". This is code for "by the time we've finished looking into it, you'll have moved on to other things and have forgotten to ask". He told BBC Surrey: "One vehicle seems to have caused mayhem but there's also an issue about how long it took for the Surrey Police to hand back the roads to the Highways Agency." Ah, handy there are at least two other agencies to blame. "I can assure you that both myself and the secretary of state, who is of course a Surrey MP, take these matters very seriously"

All very reassuring to the local populace. Just to show he is up with the detail, Mr Baker added: "The road itself had to be re-laid. The aluminium bales from the vehicle gouged into the road and caused significant damage. The gantry was very badly affected, it was unsafe and had to be removed, so there was actually a huge amount of work caused by one vehicle." I must get a professional view from Andy tomorrow; his guys were the ones who used to do all this work. I read on to find that:

"The collision initially caused tailbacks of up to 28 miles on Friday afternoon. A Nissan Micra, a Lexus and another vehicle were involved in the incident, which happened just after 16:00 BST. The lorry driver suffered serious leg injuries and was airlifted to King's College Hospital, in south-east London. The driver of the Micra also suffered serious leg injuries, while the front seat passenger in the car suffered life-threatening injuries and was airlifted to the Royal London Hospital. The bale also hit the Lexus, leaving the driver with minor injuries. Surrey Police have appealed for witnesses to come forward."

Yikes, this sounds awful. People are practically dying and I'm worrying about getting to a golf match or feeling lucky I drive a Lexus, not a Micra. The news puts it all into perspective and reminds us how dangerous a place the motorway can be. Still, the biggest news is why it took so long to re-open. There is a big forum debate about how they could have removed the central reservation and allowed people to get away earlier. Inevitably, we only look at these things from our own point of view, feel lucky not to be involved and get about our business without further thought.

Fortunately, this kind of stoppage is not too frequent. Maybe once a year or so. Generally things get sorted out pretty quickly and people do actually get on with life. Luckily we only needed to get as far as Junction 6; tomorrow it's Junction 7 but by then it'll all have been sorted. Lucky or providential? It may not be Christmas, but today it just happens that wise men came from the east.

Blown away by a cancer survivor—or two

Day 7: *Surrey Downs with Peter T, George R & Mark C. Windy. Shot 91 (32 pts); walked 6.9 miles, lost 2 balls. Blind drives, sloping fairways, curvy greens*

I'd been intrigued by today's club since November when I'd secured a tee-time there for the Monday (it's not far from Junction 8) and the General Manager and I got into a bit of correspondence which revealed he'd been recovering from cancer himself and would be delighted to play alongside me on the day, health permitting. I'd got an offer of a tee-time elsewhere for today, albeit with a small charge attached, as it was the weekend, until one day in April somebody was going on about some course they had played where they'd walked off before the finish, they thought it was so bad. When I asked where it was, I realised I'd have to amend my plans for Sunday 7th. Other people said it was OK and I won't mention it here, but as you can imagine, I wasn't too happy. Anyway, having secured Walton Heath for the Monday, a quick email asking for a change of date at Surrey Downs did the trick and we were set up here for the Sunday. It's a Peter Alliss design, so it should be interesting. Then George got in touch.

In early May I had an interesting email from George Rothman, who had "written a book *New Angles on Golf*, published in December, while I was recovering from my cancer operation and chemotherapy." What? Most people struggle to get through chemo and this guy has written a book! What's more he is giving at least 30% of his gross receipts to Cancer Research UK. Who is this guy, I wondered, reading on: "I am a 75-year-old 7 handicap golfer, and hope to be able to enter some of your events." Wow, he plays off what? If I can still play golf at 75, I'll be happy, let alone off single figures. However, "I am a shade uncertain . . ." Well, he would be if he's recovering from cancer. Oh, no, that's not the reason, I discover: "I am a shade uncertain, as I broke my right shoulder in 3 places a few weeks ago, but hope to be normally playable by August." Yikes, this is the bionic man. He's got over cancer, fell and broken his shoulder but he'll be fine for a game in a couple of months. Not only that, he's prepared to come and flog his book at my games, organise a prize table, do book signings etc. What a guy!

So he sends me a copy of the book: I read about the 5 types of putt and learn about "some advantages of a brush with cancer"! I see the foreword is by Peter Alliss: that decides it—he must play at Surrey Downs. Maybe he can get Peter A to come and play as well. That'd make a good fourball. Actually, I nearly got to ask the man himself. He was doing a turn at *Golf Live* and I hung around for a quick word and managed to give him a Golf Against Cancer leaflet before he was whisked away by his minders. Who knows, he might have a dull moment during The Open and give it a mention on air. Well unfortunately he didn't make it on the 7th, but Mark from TSG was no less welcome in making up our team for the day.

I was lucky with the weather, passing through a torrential downpour on the way but arriving to a dry course, and the M25 showed no signs of yesterday's turmoil. I'd left in good time to have "Sunday lunch" at the club, having seen the carvery advertised on their website. It'd be my meal of the day as I'd booked to stay over tonight. As I entered the chic, modern clubhouse, I was greeted by a large board bidding me welcome and giving details of the month of golf on the M25—excellent. I headed for the bar and was just about to order lunch when in came Peter with a warm "what can we do for you?" welcome and before long I was treated to a drink and an excellent lunch on the house. I stayed off the wine as I was playing golf but I'd go back there again just for the food. Nothing was too much trouble and anything I needed was sorted. He came back bearing a pile of cash he'd collected from the Saturday swindle whom he'd told about my plans and I really felt they'd taken me fully on board for the day. George joined us, giving us all copies of his book, and I bumped into Mark in the car-park, so we were ready to go.

On a course with a good number of blind drives it is always good to have some local knowledge and Peter led the way with a steady swing, firing much lower than his 16 handicap, but George was clearly the senior man and hit virtually every fairway with a compact swing and the minimum of effort as I repeatedly sliced into the rough and, with Mark, brought up the rear. We played a game called "The Chair" which is a kind of skins game where it is very hard to win points, but it worked well with our varying levels of ability. Off the tee there were just too many blind drives for me. A marker pole is OK if you hit the ball 180 yards to the middle of the fairway, but if you hit it 280 onto a sloping lie, who knows where it will end up? So I basically lost the plot here and really struggled in the wind. The greens were slick and so curvaceous that a 3-putt was almost a good result on a number of them. I'd always thought of Mr Alliss as a rather benign fellow and this very open course didn't seem to hold many dangers at first glance, but it could be very nasty if you got it wrong, which I regularly did. Fortunately today, most of my lost balls were provisionals. Needless to say, George showed us all how to play golf, with hardly a murmur of complaint despite what was clearly still quite a stiff shoulder. And we finished with an audience as Peter's wife came out in a buggy to cheer us home.

Time was getting on as I collected up the banners and jars and I was glad I'd arranged to stay just down the road, as we had an early start tomorrow at Walton Heath. Then I remembered the other jar I'd left with the folk at North Downs. It had seemed a good idea at the time, but now it was another hour at the end of the day that I felt too exhausted to embark on, having been buffeted by a howling gale all afternoon. I made the round trip on autopilot, the clubhouse was still open, I picked up the jar with 30 quid or so in it and came back in the dark to check into the Premier Inn and collapse into the bath before making a start on my homework for the night. Money raised £161.73, shots taken 91, ballzz lozzzt 2zzzzzzzzzzzzz bump and I'm asleep on the desk. No blog tonight I fear.

I've done a week now and I'm absolutely knackered. OK, it was a hell of a windy day: you knew you'd been out there. Still I've got to keep this up for another three weeks plus. I'm not sure that's going to happen. I trawl the positives: I'm going to play one of the top tracks in the country tomorrow, I'm doing this for charity and I've just been whipped on the course by two guys who've beaten cancer, so how can I complain? I could have done a lot worse with my summer, like working or going camping in the wet. No, Trevor, take a leaf out of the cancer survivors' manual: keep going and you'll live to fight another day, though the chances of playing like a 7 handicapper when I'm fifty-something, let alone 75, with or without a broken shoulder, have very much gone with the wind.

Ryder Cup lost amongst the heather

Day 8: *Walton Heath (Old Course) with Andy P, John O'C, & Bob A. Windy, occasional heavy shower. Shot 94 (28 pts); walked 7.9 miles, lost 2 balls. Superb heathland with Ryder Cup heritage.*

No need to take on the M25 today as the club's only 5 minutes away, so rather than fork out for wifi at the hotel, I'll get on down there and have a coffee in the oak-pannelled Renshaw Room whilst my partners tangle with the traffic. There is a curious mixture of modernity with tradition as I get out the laptop in such august surroundings, like using the telephone in Downton Abbey perhaps, but it's somehow calming to be in what feels almost like a gentleman's country residence. Actually ladies are allowed too, though I see they have their own separate entrance. Hmm, that might be worth looking into—well, not literally, obviously.

Plenty of time to relax and look out over the gorgeous putting green. Unusually surrounded by flower beds, it looks more like the manicured lawn of some elegant country house and I can't wait to get out there and test the surface, but we might be delayed today as Bob has been ill and has had to go to the doctor. My Club Captain, he's recently had a triple heart by-pass, so I'm just hoping he's OK. Alongside today again will be Andy, cancer recoverer and now Club Champion (net) following the recent improvement in his golfing form. My fourth is fellow Irishman John and we decide to take on this formidable partnership in an Ireland versus England derby. John hits a nice steady short ball on the fairway, so he'll make up for my wild long ball in the rough—or more likely heather as we're in the heart of Surrey heathland here.

England vs Ireland.

More like an inland links than anything else, Walton Heath features in the World's top 100 courses, outranked in the UK only by the best Open venues. It's a must-play and I nearly missed it out. My initial website enquiry fell on deaf ears and my follow-up email bounced back to me. It was only in March when I picked up the phone and spoke to the secretary direct that he gave me the proper Email address and responded, without hesitation, to my request. Not bad, given it's £145 a shout if you just turn up here. This game had filled up immediately, with my discerning partners opting for a top course before it went public. We'd been looking forward to it since then as one of the potential highlights of the tour, not a venue we'd be able to visit perhaps in the normal run of things as it doesn't put itself about for society or corporate golf. It doesn't need to.

Taking our tea in the Braid Room, we surveyed the Captain's board, noting the 1935 incumbent, no less than the Prince of Wales, who became King Edward VIII during his captaincy year. I'm sure my own club captain expects a less eventful year and fortunately the doc sees him quickly and he's on his way to join us. Shortly we're out on that lovely lawn in the sunshine and ready to go. The pro's tip is "better a short ball on the fairway than a long one in the heather" so I can see I'll need John to perform today against the old enemy, as both Andy and Bob are tidy players.

It's yours truly however who gets things straightest off the first tee on a long par 3. We wonder what Tom Watson took here as we reach for a rescue club to make the green. He was here only last week for the Senior British Open; we could have come and watched for nothing. It would have helped a lot as, though the fairways were actually pretty wide, everywhere else is covered in heather. It looks lovely, but it's the devil to get out of. Actually you can play out of it—trust me, I had plenty of practice—but nowhere have I played where the fairway wasn't more of a better option. Chipping out for 2 where I could and still behind my partner's second down the middle, I wish I could have persuaded myself to abandon the driver, but, with nearly 6,800 yards to cover from the white tees, everything would be a par 5 if you didn't have a go at it.

In between shots you are wandering amongst glorious terrain: nature tamed only enough to show you the way round, not to hold your hand here. Pleasing on the eye, tough on the swing. Today's torrential downpour arrived on the 9th and it was only when it stopped we realised that the motorway was just over the trees alongside. After 2 holes of swishing traffic we got immersed again in the beauty and the demands of the landscape before us. Honours about even on the 18th thanks to John's steady play, I decide to make up for my errant ways by spanking the ball with world record speed. It goes deep into the heather a mere few yards away to the left, I replace it with another and come in admitting I have been roundly beaten by one of the best courses in the country. John comes in with 35 points or something, but the English flag hangs over the podium today, as is perhaps only fitting in this most royal field of battle.

Over tea inside we learn more of the history of the place. Owned in the 50s and 60s by the News of The World, when that now defunct journal favoured a different kind of hacking, it hosted the first Ryder Cup featuring a European team on home soil in 1981. Against one of the best US teams ever, our boys lost 18½—9½. I wonder how many fairways they found? Not as many perhaps as Sir Ernest Holderness, who won the club's Gold Medal 18 times between 1922 and 1949: he must have been some amateur golfer. Lloyd George and Winston Churchill played here (though not together) in the days when MPs had time to play golf and didn't have all those tedious expenses forms to fill in. Dukes of Windsor and York were honorary members in their time. All of this gives the whole place an air of grandeur; it's a pity my golf was more Dukes of Hazzard than York today, but I've still had a great day and it was a real privilege to follow such footsteps across the heath.

Back on the road, I'm home pretty swiftly and sorting out my things. Not too much cash in the jar today, but with £300 raised from the golf, it's been the best fundraising day so far. I'm just going to update my stats when I realise I've lost a folder with all my admin. OK, I can print some of it off again, but there was Bob's cheque for £100, sweepstake entries, cash and other stuff in there. I phone the club but they are closed by now, so I leave a message. I'm sure it's the kind of place it'd get handed in. I ask the hotel to get the cleaners to have a look: I'm going back that way in the morning so I can always call in. I make a little checklist of "things not to forget." Just going to bed I notice there's a message on my ansaphone: it's Walton Heath housekeeping saying they've got my stuff. I phone the hotel and say not to worry. Too overawed by the environment to pay attention to essential detail off the course as well as on it, I guess, or just too tired after another day in the wind and rain, I shut down for the day and fall asleep dreaming of the heather where not only was the Ryder Cup lost but two of my Srixons lie hidden away forever.

TREVOR SANDFORD

A tough ask for the ladies

Day 9: *Tyrrells Wood Golf Club with Andy P, John M & Diana B. Sunny, light breeze. Shot 92 (31 pts); walked 7.2 miles, lost 3 balls. Scenic, hilly, tough for the ladies.*

It's my daughter Helena's birthday today so I've been thinking about things from a female perspective. She's miffed that I'm PLAYING GOLF AGAIN on her special day, but I've agreed to be home in time to serve drinks at the "pre-lash" before she and her girlie friends hit the clubs for the evening. In fact, I've even offered to give a lift over from Surrey to some of her Uni friends, providing they can make their way to the golf club. How's that for fatherly service?

There's been an accident today so traffic's a bit slow but I have Andy for company so we argue about which lane *is* the quickest at junction 5, why they ever used concrete for the road surface and how "hard shoulder running" will work on the "managed motorway" in the future. Oh the joys of blokey conversation: James May could make a series out of this.

Nipping in to Walton Heath to pick up my folder, I notice the discreet sign indicating *Ladies' entrance* and wonder how that goes down. Do they feel privileged to be allowed access, or condemned as second-class citizens? I've not looked into it, so who knows, they may have superior toiletries for all I know. Certainly the men's locker room was very much like a gentleman's club, with Old Spice and Brylcreem on tap, all overseen by a watchful steward.

Anyway, there are women about, so they must be OK with it all. I did hear of one club which I'm visiting later on the tour where some ladies complained that a man was heard to swear after missing a putt on the final green in the Sunday Medal whilst they were watching from the terrace. The complaint went all the way to the committee who came up with an innovative solution—ladies are now banned from the terrace at the weekend.

Onward through wooded lanes and private roads to the stunning clubhouse at Tyrrells Wood, a rambling Victorian pile which sits atop a hill looking out over the world around. With a westerly aspect, the terrace must be one of the prime "gin and tonic" spots in all of Surrey, the perfect place for a sundowner with the other half. I expect ladies are not banned from here. Well, let's hope not as today we have our first and only female TSGer joining us. Alongside me, Andy and John we have Diana, a relatively recent convert to golf from hockey who plays off a 34 handicap. We play *The Chair* as it's a good option for such a diverse group, rather than the more uneven matchplay format.

I've been warned it's a hilly course and we follow a big society as they launch their tee-shots off the first into what seems like a bottomless chasm. With my length off the tee I could even drive the green—or end up on the next fairway, which is what I did. After a bit of a blow-out on the tricky 2nd (blind drive again), I settle a bit and get some control of my swing. Only four bad holes spoil the card and I get in with 31 points which doesn't feel too bad. I even magic up the shot of the week—a 6-iron, fired 178 yards completely blind over trees to 10 feet under the pin from practically the next fairway. That Seve-style recovery saved a par on the Stroke Index 1, making it feel like an easy hole!

Meanwhile, Diana's plugging away at it from the ladies tees and I notice something a bit odd about them. Normally the blokes play off yellow or white tee-markers and the ladies go from red markers on a separate tee-ing ground that's often up to 100 yards nearer the hole. A reasonable compensation for their generally lesser physical strength, perhaps, unless it's a longest drive competition and you're playing against Laura Davies. Here, however, nearly all of the red markers seem to be set on the same tee-box as the yellows, just a few yards in front. On the par-5 12th, for instance, it's a tough ask for a decent male golfer to get the 520 yards up hill to the green in three strokes, but the ladies have all of 490 yards to do the same. Maybe they do have female members here, but they must all be Olympic athletes . . .

Then there's that other aspect of a round of golf that separates the men from the ladies. What to do with all that water you've drunk? Whilst there are plenty of trees about, most ladies prefer to wait till the turn and pop into the clubhouse. For courses where the 9th hole doesn't come back home, it's a different matter and there are sometimes handy huts and half-way houses with appropriate facilities. I've even seen portaloos on some courses. Here, unfortunately, it is a bit of a trek up to the clubhouse at the turn and then you find the ladies' cloakrooms are *upstairs*! Not very convenient. I wonder if anyone has ever put this to the committee.

At last we're on the 18th tee and the clubhouse looms again into view, bathed in late afternoon sunshine. I can definitely feel a cool beer coming on, followed by a glass of Marlborough Sauvignon, a few olives and maybe . . . wake up, Trevor, you're playing golf AND you have to drive home. Oh yes and I have a couple of young ladies to pick up too; the drinks will have to wait until later. I close out with a par and bounce up the steps where Lucy and Emma are waiting. I'll have to come back another day with time to linger; today we've got to load up and hit the road. My daughter's drinks party awaits and I'm under orders to get them there by 7.

So whilst the ladies seem to have got the upper hand in controlling our behaviour *off* the course, it seems that some clubs are quite content to make them pay back *on* the course, whether that be by giving them their own special entrance or by simply making the course so hard to play they'll come back next time without the clubs and just enjoy the view. I'm sure it isn't deliberate, but I do wonder how many white wine spritzers ever get served on *this* sundowner terrace.

The strain begins to show

Day 10: *Burhill Golf Club (New Course) with Richard A, Graham N & Kamal. Windy, bright. Shot 97 (25 pts); walked 7 miles, lost 4 balls. Undiscovered gem.*

I have concluded that Thursday is the quietest day for golf. Believe me, I've tried them all over the years. It's hard to say why but no-one seems to want to take the day off and then have to go back to the office on Friday; much better to work late on Thursday, take Friday off and catch up on Monday. Maybe that explains why, in the last week of July, Burhill, despite being an Open qualifier with a very expensive-looking ambience, remained unbooked. My wife sent out a missive to her whole address-book whilst I was away and Richard came back with an offer to join me "in the interests of Trevor not having to play alone." Graham had also made the same commitment. I didn't tell either of them when Kamal signed up on 31st August, so in the end I had a fourball and, better still, Richard offered to drive.

That was the first sign of strain relieved—someone else would get me there. I'd only been on the M25 proper for a few days but already it was getting to be quite an enterprise leaving early enough to make sure I got there on time and got everything done, as well as getting home again too. On the way, Richard asked if I'd done any special preparation for the month of golf and I had to confess that I hadn't really. Well, OK, I'd been going to Pilates classes for the past 6 months in the belief that they'd improve my core strength and stability and I'd had a couple of lessons with my home club pro to help me try to play more conservatively: clearly I was having difficulty applying his advice on the course!

It's been ten days now, though, and the strain is beginning to show. I wake up with a sore back every morning; maybe it's age or something, but it tends to loosen up when I get going so I haven't bothered much about it. However today for the first time, I've given in and taken Ibuprofen. One of today's apparent wonder drugs, it seems to seek out the source of pain and help you forget about it whilst you're playing. I don't want to become an addict but I now have a box of 400mg tablets in my bag at all times.

Actually, it's not so much the arms and legs that are the problem. If you can walk and swing your arms around you can play golf, though don't quote me on that as I know there is a bit more to it. No, it's the points of contact with the outside world you have to worry about: hands and feet, basically. On the third day, I was having difficulty gripping my club in the boiling heat. One of my playing partners, John, was a leftie and I asked him if he'd got a spare right hand glove. Delving deep into his golf bag, he found a discarded one. Let's say it had seen better days, but I gave it a go and it helped so much that I went off and got a new one which I've been wearing ever since. I don't even take it off to putt. It doesn't wear out as fast as the left one, but it has stopped me getting a blister on my right ring finger, which otherwise was starting to trouble me. Sometimes I'd used a plaster as well, but the glove seems to work in prevention. Now I'll never get the prestigious "Golfer's tan" (right hand brown, left hand pale), but if it keeps me going for the month, who cares?

And then there are the feet. Helena's a medical student who has worked in a pharmacy for three years, so I turn to her for professional advice and emerge with a special pack of blister plasters and a preventative stick, a bit like lip balm, but bigger. You rub it on the areas you think are going to get blistered and it sort of lubricates them, reducing chafing etc. Well of course it takes a few days to know which bits are going to be affected so you have to get the timing right and not leave it too late. So far, I'm doing OK. But then also I've bought a couple of extra pairs of golf shoes. My plan was to rotate them over 3 days, but currently I'm just using two on odds and evens. If one of them does rub, then at least I may have a day to recover whist the other one rubs somewhere else. Oh and did I say I'm also wearing two pairs of socks (one thin, one thick)? It just seemed like a good idea—more cushioning I thought. So with two gloves and two pairs of socks now, by the end of the month I could be covered in layers of clothing!

Actually the fairways of the New Course at Burhill were so good it was like walking on carpet. It's a well-laid out track that is proving quite a challenge in the wind, longer and more open than its older sister course. Why has no-one I know ever played here? It's an excellent venue with a fabulous Georgian mansion for a clubhouse and there really is hardly anyone about. Where are the good people of Walton-on-Thames, I wonder? Probably on the 7.14 to Waterloo, I imagine, and already hard at work at their city desks. Out here, we've got a strong wind blowing and I'm struggling to get off the tee, though I do par the hardest holes, making a mockery of the stroke index with my inconsistency. I guess there are so many great golfing venues nearby that this is just another one to some, but for the four of us it was "a very agreeable day out." As for the fundraising, nobody at the bar means no money in the jar but one generous benefactor gives me a cheque for far more than I was expecting and today's takings top the table at £300, which will take some beating.

Just a pity my golf didn't quite rise to the same dizzy heights. Maybe that's the other dimension of the strain beginning to show, with energy levels, stamina and so on. My ever-resourceful wife has now provided me with a continuous supply of Cornish pasties, pork pies and fruity flapjacks, so I need never fear low blood sugar on the course. After the first few scorching days, I've learned to bring plenty of water. I just get tired in the evening and if I don't sleep in the car on the way home, which is not recommended if driving, I certainly sleep at night, but then this is what the human body has evolved for—going out hunting, not sitting at a computer. I've actually lost 3 lbs over the first week but am feeling fitter when I'm out there. Maybe I've got to some kind of plateau where I can keep going almost indefinitely? That's where I've got to look out and make sure some incautious blister or stupid muscle twinge doesn't get in the way. Otherwise, I'm good to go for a few days yet. I'm surviving the strain which is great because I'm now stretching the elastic a bit to get home every night and from tomorrow, I'm going to be staying away. That'll mean I'm well and truly "on the road" and I'm nearly a third of the way round. Who knows, I might just make it after all.

TREVOR SANDFORD

Bad golfer gets Star treatment.

Day 11: Foxhills (Bernard Hunt Course) with Andy P, John O'C & Bob R. Cloudy. Shot 100 (23 pts); walked 7.4 miles, lost 3 balls. Pretty but no walk in the park.

By my last day in Surrey, I've become quite accustomed to pulling up through iron gates onto the long drive through the trees towards the impressive country mansion, so, in a way, today is no different. However, they have a hotel and spa here so Andy has booked in to stay over with the wife for a bit of pampering afterwards. My other half is still clearing up after my daughter's party and declines the offer (at least that's one version of the story) and anyway I've arranged to stay with Tesh, my mate from the village who works up here during the week and has a pad in Walton-on-Thames. Unfortunately he was working away last night so I'm going there today instead. I'll be home tomorrow so I'm not fully "on the road" yet, but it's a good trial run.

Just as well because, in my rush to depart today, I've come without two essential items: the battery for my electric trolley and, more seriously, my wallet. Oh well, I can probably cadge a few quid off someone until the weekend but by the look of the terrain around here, I'll not be carrying my clubs, so I'll definitely need a trolley. By the pro-shop I bump into Sean, via whom my tee-time has been arranged, and he sorts everything out for me, in a style I haven't experienced for a few days now. Of course you can have one of our motocaddies, no charge, do have a course planner and I'll get the ground staff to put up those banners for you—where would you like them? Star treatment indeed.

Over coffee John and I agree to another Ireland-England match against Andy and Bob, though it's a different Bob this time, an occasional golfer I meet once a year on our trip to Portugal. Maybe we have more of a chance today but Bob is remarkably consistent for a man who plays about 5 times a year and my hope may be misplaced. Actually I am the architect of my own undoing today as over the past 10 days I have acquired an unhelpful combination of characteristics off the tee—greater distance and less accuracy. The ball is going miles and this is a tight course. The scene is set on the 2nd when after a 290-yard drive I follow up with the first shank Andy has ever seen me hit. I put the dreaded lob wedge away after that; I should have done the same with the driver. On the 16th, John remarks that it's the first hole where he hasn't had to help me find my ball! The course proves long and tough for him too and it's not going to be a good day for the boys in green.

Still, the round has been eventful and no easy walk in the park. On the par-3 4th a buggy rolls up as I take my second shot from amongst the trees to reach the green. It's a photographer looking for the M25 man to get a snap for the club's monthly newsletter. Two shots later I make it onto the short grass and they take me sinking a putt, or maybe it was pretending to sink it. With a run of two triple bogeys and three doubles, they'd have plenty of shots to choose from, 34 of them in 5 holes! I'll be lucky to break 100 at this rate.

It wasn't just me who was playing bad golf, though. There's a nice little halfway house behind the ninth green and we decided to pull in there for refreshments before tackling the 10th. We were just paying for the tea when suddenly a ball shot through the open doorway and clattered all over the room at very high speed, narrowly missing china, glass and golfers and luckily causing no damage. Looking back down the ninth, it appears that someone else thins their lob wedges too. We offer him the chance to play through on the basis that he's in a buggy but more for our own safety and he declines. Now we're going to have to play the back nine with hard hats on.

Andy's wife Heather had walked the front nine with us, taking copious photographs but decided now was a good time to seek out the safety and comfort of the spa so off she went. A good move as today's torrential downpour came on the 13th. Unlucky for some. After that the golf improved very slightly with only one more triple bogey and even two pars, but I'm afraid I didn't manage to keep it to double figures and needless to say the emerald isle did not win the day. At least the winnings will go into the charity jar, so it's just a matter of who pays.

We get in and Heather has some good news for me. She's had a word with the people in the spa and guess what? They are so taken by the madness of playing golf for a month that they have offered me a complimentary back massage after the round. How's that for star treatment? So after we've done the scores, the drinks and the well done chaps, it's into the pool for a few quick lengths to cool down and then on with the robe and slippers, not quite knowing what to expect. Well, this is a sporty kind of place so it's fairly firm with the old thumbs and elbows, but it doesn't half feel good at the end of a very tough round where I've walked twice as far as it says on the card uphill and down dale. I lie back and think of England (and how we can beat them next time) and come out feeling totally relaxed and smelling of roses—or was it lavender? Well, something flowery anyway. Another bonus is I only have a 20 minute drive to Tesh's place so no time to pick up motorway stress again.

It's a nice flat and, being basically set up for a bloke staying 4 nights a week, has plenty of beer in the fridge—but no wifi. How am I going to do my blog, I cry? The fans will be logging on in anticipation. No joke, here; we are getting plenty of hits now and people are chipping in so I have to do an update. No worries, mate, they'll have it at the pub, says Tesh, so off we go. Passing *The Swan* where we ate on my last visit, we go for *The Angler* and the first question he asks is do you have wifi? Assured by the affirmative, we sit down to eat. I order fish pie picturing in my mind the enormous portions they serve at the *Cock*

Inn in Barford, a regular haunt on our visits to Norwich. We fire up the laptop but I'm not getting a signal. Oh no, it's normally fine, says the barman, there must be a problem with the server; it'll probably be on again by the time you've had your main course. Well that's unlikely because what has just arrived looks distinctly like a starter and Tesh is beginning to doubt his choice of hostelry on more than one count. A small but tasty portion later, there is still no wifi, so we cut our losses and head back to the *Swan*, only after Tesh's tactful enquiry about portion control elicits a refund from the landlord. He's paying, obviously, as I've got no money!

We'll have pudding here, I suggest, as I see Strawberries and Cream on the board outside. But first, we'd better ask about the wifi. Oh yes we do have wifi, fine no problem. Is there a code we need or anything? Ah yes, it's on the menu, but it's just changed. Now what's the new code, does anyone know? Anyone? No? Oh dear, oh dear. Tell you what, says Tesh, I know where we can go, so we decamp without a pudding and head back to his place. Now just opposite is the Walton-on-Thames Conservative Club, of which he is a member. I am assured that the main reason for this is so that he can use their car park, which sounds good enough for me as the key thing is they *do* have wifi—he's picked up the signal from his front room! Well it's long past dinner time now, so we sit down for a drink in the corner and at last get the website up so I can show him the blog and get my updates in. Trouble is we've had more to drink than eat and I'm nodding off after a hard day at the office, so we call it a day. I'm not playing till 11 o'clock in the morning; I'm sure they'll have wifi at the clubhouse: I can do it then.

I'm actually more than a third of the way round now. I've clocked the biggest score I've had for a very long time, but I don't blame the course. I'd go there again tomorrow, with or without the massage. The golf can only improve, but the star treatment could hardly have been better.

TREVOR SANDFORD

Longest drive at Ashford

Day 12: *Ashford Manor Golf Club with John T, Ben T & Barry F. Cloud. Shot 87 (32 pts); walked 6.4 miles, lost 1 ball. Flat parkland at traditional members' club.*

I almost miss the entrance off an unremarkable suburban street and I have a bad feeling today as the iron gates say "keep out" to non-members, but as I close in they swing slowly open to permit me access. I note the keypad required to exit and follow the clear sign which points me away from the tarmac parking lot round the corner to the gravel of the Visitors' Car Park. It's a bit embarrassing to be here so early: I'm over two hours in advance of my tee-time but I do need to get online and catch up from yesterday, so I make my way into the substantial clubhouse—obviously the Manor after which the course is named—and look for the manager. They don't have specific tee times at this members' club but they sent me a voucher to present on arrival to claim my complimentary fourball. It was all set up before Christmas.

I find Peter busy in conversation with another member of staff and when I get his attention say I've a tee-time for 11 o'clock and sorry to be so early, but . . . we don't actually have tee-times here . . . Yes, I know but you may remember I booked in some time ago, I've got a fourball . . . is it in the book, I don't recall . . . yes, I have a voucher here; I'm playing all round the M25; this is day 12 and . . . oh, yes, I do vaguely remember, do you want to get out now . . . no I'm a bit early, the others are coming from Kent. I've a couple of banners I'd like to put up, with Cancer Research on them . . . actually, we'd rather you didn't;

we have a competition here later today; in fact we have a shotgun start at 5 o'clock, so the earlier you get out the better as the course will be closed . . . don't worry, we should be gone well before then . . .

So after a somewhat inauspicious start, he gives me a quick tour of the facilities, pointing out the locker room and bar etc. I casually ask if they have wi-fi . . . no, sorry we don't here . . . do you know if there's anywhere local that does? . . . afraid not, I don't live locally, I only work here, I suppose you might get something in one of the hotels in Staines perhaps. Oh and you'll need a code for the changing room and a code to get out the gate—I'll sort that out for you shortly . . . Well I have plenty of time in hand so I head off to explore the local environment looking for wi-fi. Luckily someone is walking out as I approach the gate, so he swipes his card to let me out and in a few minutes I've parked round the corner in a high street that could be virtually anywhere in suburban London. I pop into the local library. Wifi? No, sorry Sir, but I can get you a day visitor's card for £3 if you want to use one of the computers. Hmm, not really what I was after. I've got all my stuff on the laptop here and I just want to upload it. Costa Coffee doesn't have wifi either but I stumble upon a computer shop and feel they must be able to help.

Phil, who holds court from behind a desk at the back, is astonished to find anyone from outside the area actually coming to Ashford. When I tell him I'm going to the golf club he goes into a well-rehearsed diatribe about the place. His old man is a member there and it's the snottiest place around, according to Phil. People come over from the next fairway to tell you to tuck your shirt in and all that kind of stuff. I mean, it's not Wentworth here, is it? Phil continues to lambast his place of birth in colourful tones I could not repeat here but he does help me hook up to his wifi so I can get on the website and update the blog. Now, I'm not overly technical but there's something different about this and I need to download some kind of compatibility patch or something. We give up on the laptop and he lets me use one of his

TREVOR SANDFORD

computers, but it's on a different version of Word and doesn't like the memory stick I'm having to use to save my work. Now time is ticking and, despite the entertaining conversation, I do feel I've got to go, as John and the others will be arriving soon and we have to be off in time to be clear before the course closes. I'll be home tonight and I'll just have to do the blog then.

Back at the club I'm all set to go, it's 10.30 and John still isn't here. Perhaps I should give him a ring. Oh, I don't have his number, we did it all by email. John's a colleague of a friend and we only meet up once a year on our annual trip to France, so I don't know him that well, but I did bump into him with his brother-in-law Barry at the Open at Sandwich a few weeks ago and we parted with "see you at Ashford Manor", so I know he's not forgotten. I ring our mutual friend Nick, who's cycling in the New Forest but does have John's number on him so eventually at 10.40 I get through to the man himself. The rest you could not make up.

Hi John, Trevor here. Where are you, mate? . . . We're in Ashford . . . Oh, no problem, then, it's only two minutes away; do you need directions . . . Er, no mate, as I say we're in Ashford. Yes? What? No! . . . we're in Ashford, Kent! . . . John, this is day 12, junction 12 of the month of golf on the M25—there's a clue in the title there somewhere . . . Yes, I did think it was a bit odd, but I thought with all that travelling you must have wanted the odd day nearer home . . . John, I'm on the M25, mate . . . well it's OK anyway because the guy here at Ashford says we can tee off and as it's for charity he'll give us a free round so you can still have the money . . . er, that's not really the same, John, we're booked here and we're supposed to be teeing off in ten minutes. Do you think you'd be able to get here? I rest the phone for a few minutes whilst John consults with his son and brother-in-law and decides what to do. The phone rings: "We're on our way" and a quick calculation says it's about 80 miles and probably an hour and a half with a following wind. If we're lucky we'll get out before 1 o'clock and if we're quick we'll be finished by 5.

Meanwhile the secretary wonders why I'm still hanging around and when I explain my dilemma we get a whole series of "wrong Ashford" stories, including lorries delivering tonnes of turf and so on. Thoughts of "didn't you tell him where to go" are clearly flickering through his mind. In order to look busy, I go and get a coffee and then get out a pad and start writing today's blog. So much to say already, I might as well get ahead with it, so I park myself on a bench by the starter's hut and watch as the members roll up in their mid-morning groups and take to the first tee. People don't usually sit around waiting here, so I have to explain what I'm up to and air my own "wrong Ashford" story. It gets better with the telling, though no less embarrassing, but at least they are now all aware of the Month of Madness and maybe that'll pay dividends when they see the charity jar in the bar later.

Just after 12.30 a car pulls up and the boys have got here, probably breaking most of the speed limits on the way. We have a quick "how did this happen?" conversation and get on the tee. Barry wears a wicked grin and clearly John won't be allowed to forget about this for a while. Without more ado we get off and away and actually the golf isn't too bad. Lucky really, as they don't have a strokesaver and my GPS watch packs up—clearly another problem with the charging connector. The course looks nice and is completely flat which is handy as I'm pushing my trolley around with no battery. Can anything else go wrong? Just forget it and get on with the golf, I tell myself.

Somebody calls over from a nearby tee. I see we all have our shirts tucked in so wonder if it's Ben's trainer socks they are going to object to: he's a young lad and ankle socks are just not the look for his age group. To my surprise they start asking directions—word has clearly got around about today's *faux pas*—and we all have a laugh about geography. Eventually the skies clear, the sun shines and we get in well ahead of the 5 o'clock curfew. A quick shower and we're on the terrace having a drink. I tell them what Phil has said about the club and notice that Ben's socks have completely gone now and he's wearing flip-flops;

TREVOR SANDFORD

yes, he says, someone just said to him "You're lucky, as it's after 5 now." Apparently on Friday evening the dress code relaxes and you can get away *without socks*! Some guys on the next table are having a mock argument with the manager about it and pretending they are about to take their socks off as the clock chimes. At least they can see the funny side of it, but to be honest what difference does it make whether you wear socks before or after 5 or not? These are just the kind of rules that get up Phil's nose and create the impression he has of the club. They are also a headache for me as I'm depending on their hospitality and feel responsible for the behaviour of my entourage. Today, however, it was just good to get out on the course with anybody in the end, I didn't even think about how they were dressed.

The course is now full with a shotgun start and the bar will be teeming later. Where are you playing tomorrow, asks the steward? Laleham—well that's just down the road; why don't you leave your jar with us and we'll see if we can't raise a bit more for you from the crowd tonight? I take them up on the offer and head off, grasping a piece of paper with the exit code so I can get out the gates on my own this time. An hour and a half later I'm home and I realise why it was sensible to stay over and will be again from tomorrow onwards. It's been a long week and I'm not playing until 2pm tomorrow, so I'll do all my admin in the morning: time to have a night off. I reacquaint myself with my wallet and head out to the pub. At the bar someone recognises me from the article about the tour in the local paper and asks me how it's going. She gets the "wrong Ashford" story, as does more or less everyone I meet for the next few days. You really couldn't have made it up. I've had a fair hack back to Kent from West London, but it's John who definitely gets the prize for the Longest Drive today.

Slice of life on both sides of the river

Day 13: Laleham Golf Club with Dougie G, Dave F & John B. Warm, overcast. Shot 89 (32 pts); walked 6 miles, lost 4 balls. Relaxed, cheerful, cheap.

Oh, you're at Laleham tomorrow—that's just down the road, said the man at the bar at Ashford Manor. Checking the map I saw he was right—Laleham village lies on the north bank of the Thames about 3 miles away. However the golf course is on the south bank and the local geography of rivers and lakes means that both clubs are most easily reachable via Junction 13. I'd used junction 12 yesterday, so it would be 13 today, thus preserving the sense of order of my M25 circumnavigation. As ever, though, the motorway had other ideas and when it came to it, I turned off at junction 11 and made my way through Chertsey. I'd done this journey many times, because the road leading to today's venue turns off just opposite Thorpe Park, site of many a summer birthday party for one of my daughters. Today there were no screaming teenagers, just me and my clubs as I headed through rather less prestigious surroundings than most of last week: no iron gates at all here, but you have to get through a caravan park to find the course. It's tempting to give up as it feels like you must be wrong but a small sign confirms you are on the right track and shortly you're parked a few yards from the river near what looks like a Victorian cricket pavilion.

Though this was one of the cheapest venues on the tour, I'd only managed to negotiate the members' guest rate when the itinerary was agreed, so I remembered my wallet today and had cash at the ready. However John in the pro shop would have none of it. His mother died from cancer a few years ago and anyone supporting cancer research could of course have a concession. That was great as we had a fourball again today, made up entirely of TSG members who'd signed up for a slice of the month of madness. Wandering round in my conspicuous *Golf Against Cancer* royal blue, I soon gathered up my playing partners, Dougie, Dave and John, who'd come from Surrey, Berkshire and Bedfordshire to join me. John was halfway through a panini in the newly refurbished clubhouse when we had to get on the tee, but the barmaid found him some aluminium foil and out it came with him, too tasty to leave behind.

I'd decided that after yesterday's dress code anxieties, this was a course where I could wear my cargo shorts with pride, so I was surprised to see a big sign laying out the dress code in detail:

Dress code

Well I needn't have worried, unless of course I'd worn a suit and tie, which is my normal "workwear", but then that would perhaps pass as "smart dress" so might be OK. I get the general drift, though. This is clearly a club which welcomes casual play but doesn't want people just turning up off the building site at the end of a hot day and sticking on a pair of trainers to hack round the course. It's a proper golf club, so you need to dress accordingly. My M&S cargo shorts will be absolutely fine.

Though right next to the Thames, you don't see the river at all from the course; there are a couple of ponds, though otherwise it's dry, courtesy of the drainage system created in the 7th century by the monks of Chertsey Abbey (wonderful what you can read about in the strokesaver sometimes!). A flock of geese crosses our path on a couple of the greens and you do have to be a bit careful when cleaning your ball, but the main feature today is that the greens have just been treated—tined and sanded, though not yet mown, so they are both gritty and hairy and you have to give the ball a great thump for it to go any distance. Yesterday the club details announced that "we can boast some of the finest greens in Middlesex that have continued to perplex some of the countries scratch golfers". Today, I'm going to be far more perplexed, scratching my head to work out how to avoid three-putting. I'm sure the greens will be perfect in a few weeks, and decent enough in days, but it's just too bad they did them yesterday and we're here today. Luck of the draw, I suppose. I see now why Sunningdale, which can no doubt afford to do so, closes for a week in the summer whilst this is going on—one reason I'm not there today.

Dougie suggests we play *Animals* which is a good format for a mixed bunch who've never played together before. A three-putt earns a *snake*, finding a bunker a *camel* and into the woods or out of bounds a *gorilla*. Popping the ball into water earns you a *frog* and a *pig* is awarded by general agreement if a shot is just too awful. The animal gets passed around to the latest person to earn it, so it gets a bit more crucial towards the end of the round. Soon we are treading amongst the geese bearing camels and snakes and I've got at least two gorillas.

TREVOR SANDFORD

In the pairs match we're playing alongside, I'm giving away shots to the guys here and still trying to bash the ball too hard in my efforts to keep up. Dougie proves too good and Dave has a very nice draw for a 28 handicapper so despite John's valiant efforts, we lose the pairs and I pick up most of the wildlife. On the last I'm stuck up against a tree and have to play out left-handed. That done, I find myself in thick grass and chunk a lob wedge out of there at speed onto the patio. There's a wedding reception inside and the photographer was taking a restful break until I got near. Fortunately he doesn't get the shot and I don't zoom in on him, but I do lose the last of 4 balls of the afternoon, most of them over the hedge and far away.

Inside for a drink afterwards, the bar's quiet but it's really buzzing in the dining room where the wedding is in full swing. They're a lively crowd who know how to enjoy themselves. When we do have to go, I head up to the bar to collect the sweetie jar with today's charity takings and it is nowhere to be seen. Sorry, mate, says the barman, I've had to put it away with all these people coming back and forth from the wedding and so on. Someone's already nicked your newspaper article and I didn't want the same thing to happen to the cash in the jar! (Oh well, there is still some in there.) Maybe you could leave it with us for tomorrow; we'll be full of members then and could probably collect a lot more. I do give this due consideration, but I don't really fancy retracing my steps every day for the promise of a few quid more and decide to cut my losses and move on. I've still got to get back to Ashford Manor tonight to pick up yesterday's donations.

It's a twelve-mile trek around via Staines to do the 3 miles across the Thames. Passing Thorpe Park you can still hear the screams from *Stealth* and the rumbles from *Nemesis* as the kids enjoy themselves south of the river. Back on the other side, it's all much more civilised as there's some kind of dinner on at the golf club and the dining room is full of people in blazers, club ties and so on. I suddenly feel completely out of place in my cargo shorts, but I'm only here for the money, so

I seek out the barman and ask for the sweetie-jar. Ah yes, here it is, says John. We had a good crowd in today and I must say Mary and Jan did a great job arm-twisting—nobody got away from the bar without making a contribution. I pick it up and practically drop it again—the thing is two-thirds full and weighs a ton, with hundreds of coins and a good many notes as well. That'll take some counting when I eventually get home. I thank everyone profusely and head out via the locker-room exit towards the car park. Just then I bump into the guy from the patio yesterday afternoon. Oh how did you get on today, he asks, seeing the jar in my hands. Actually I did put something in there earlier, but it wasn't a lot, he adds as he reaches for his wallet and puts in another tenner.

So as West London parties, at the disco on the south bank and the dining table on the north, I reflect on suburban life here in this corner of Surrey which stretches into what was once called Middlesex and think there is nothing "middling" about it at all. It may just be the luck of the draw but I've experienced a slice of life on both sides of the river that couldn't be more different. I've had fun on the south side and could have joined the party if I hadn't been racing home tonight. My casual dress wouldn't have got me into the dining room north of the river, but when I get home and tip out the contents of the sweetie-jar, I'm counting for ages before the total comes in at £269.67 This is about ten times what I've come to expect of a day's takings at the bar. I'm reflecting on my IT friend Phil's views on the people of this establishment, but as far as generosity is concerned I won't have a word said against them. Even my cargo shorts hadn't big enough pockets to take away the money they raised for me today.

TREVOR SANDFORD

Golf is not subject to the laws of physics.

Day 14: *Datchet Golf Club with Tony G. Sunny evening. Shot 85 (37 pts); walked 6.2 miles, lost 3 balls. Good little 9-holer.*

Junction 14 was always a challenge. Surrounded by reservoirs and right next to Heathrow, it's not exactly your first choice location for a golf course. The nearest courses to here are much nearer other junctions, too far out into the country, or too far into town; there really aren't many options. Windsor boasts both the Eton College and the Royal Household Golf Clubs but not being an old boy or on matey enough terms with the Duke of York, I won't be getting into either of these. But, hey, what's that I see on the satellite map, squeezed up between the railway line and the river—it's Datchet Golf Club. A nine-hole course with something like 15 different tees, it looks decent enough from the website and should be worth a go. Sorry, Sir, Sunday we'll be chock-a-block with members, we'd like to help, but . . . is the secretary's not unexpected reply. Well how about later on in the day—4pm, even; there'll still be plenty of light? So it's settled and my only 9-holer goes on the itinerary, making it also the only course in Berkshire on the roster. For the M25 geeks, the royal county hosts the motorway for less than half a mile, next to Runnymede (which is in Surrey, just to be awkward), so it is in fact more than adequately represented . . .

Thing is, not many people want to play on a Sunday evening and, despite my protestations of its quality, a nine-hole course just isn't proving a sufficient incentive. Looks like I'll definitely be going round solo, unless they maybe pair me up with a member. I'm about to cash in my "I'll play with you if you are really stuck" card a couple of days beforehand when Tony signs up via TSG. Living in Hampshire and working in Essex during the week, it's actually on his way to work, as it were, and he might as well break the journey with a game of golf as at a motorway service station.

Today, I'm fully packed up and "on the road" as we are now too far away from home for daily commuting and I'll not be back for nearly a fortnight. I hope I haven't forgotten anything as I find my B&B just 100 yards away from junction 13, sign in, dump my stuff and head out for the golf course. At the end of a short street of tidy Edwardian villas, I suddenly find myself in the car park and I'm there. The pro is still about, well into his post-round tipple in the bar, but he's expecting me and says he'll rattle the tin for me as the members come in. I meet up with Tony on the tee and we're away.

On the first, we are caught up by the last group of members playing through for their back 9, so we let them through, hoping it'll now be clear behind. How's it going, I casually ask one as he passes. It's my first day back on the course after chemotherapy, is his unexpected reply and in our very brief exchange I establish that Ian's been through it just like my mate Andy. I've got something you might like, I find myself saying, and make a mental note to pop into the clubhouse at the turn. We play on, the rescue club/lob wedge combination serving me well so I am one under gross after four holes. The evening sun casts long shadows across the green and it's great to be out there on a warm summer evening. I'm hoping Ian will enjoy many more of these.

Then at the 8th, I make the mistake of asking Tony what he does. He's a high energy physicist, as it happens, and it turns out we read the subject at the same university, albeit three years apart and many, many years ago. He was probably in lectures with my other half. I'm thinking of coincidences and chaos theory rather than how to get off the tee and make double bogey, but come back immediately at the blind par-3 9th with a chip-in birdie, against all the laws of probability. I'm round in 37 shots, 2 over gross and by far the best golf I've played on the tour. I pop to the car and dig out one of George Rothman's books: I feel moved to give it to Ian as an encouragement to maintain his fight back and I find him in the bar to pass it on. How's it going, says the pro, now even further into relaxation mode. Oh, a couple over, I casually remark and see him look in disbelief that a 13-handicapper can be burning up his course so easily.

Can't rely on the laws of physics here.

Now on the 10th tee, Heisenberg's uncertainty principle takes over. To the uninitiated, this states that it is impossible to predict with any degree of accuracy both the position and momentum of a particle. Translated into golf, this means I can tell where I've hit the ball but not how far. Suddenly instead of walking down the middle of the fairway towards my ball, I am looking for it aimlessly in the hedge. When I do find it behind some trees, I discover wave-particle duality at work. This means that whilst we might normally think of a golf ball as obeying

Newton's Laws of motion in a predictable sense, bouncing off wood and passing through gaps, it seems that my ball now has wave-like properties. Thus, instead of passing unfettered through the space between the trees, it undergoes diffraction, spreading out into a whole range of possible positions, rather as the sound from the TV does as is passes through the door into the next room, round corners and up the stairs etc. This is a very worrying phenomenon. Chaos reigns as I complete my random walk in the park: quantum fluctuation results in highly unpredictable outcomes and I'm coming away with 7s and 9s rather than the tidy pars of the previous circuit. Even the putting is impossible as I experience interference on the fringes. Why did we ever start to talk about physics instead of just playing golf?

To those for whom the previous paragraph has made no sense whatsoever, I would say please read my as yet unpublished monograph *The role of uncertainty in Golf* which argues the case for a paradigm shift in thinking about golf at the atomic level. I guess I've lost everybody now. Let's just say it gives you another excuse, and a totally unintelligible one at that, for playing badly. I add a 48 to my earlier 37 to yield an unremarkable 85, just a couple over my handicap. It won't show on the card today, but the laws of physics have taken a new turn and I've got no idea what's going to happen next on the golf course. If nothing else, the weeks ahead are going to be fun!

It's well after dark now as we hit the bar before leaving; even the pro has called it a day. I pick up the sweetie-jar, which hasn't done badly for a small club. I don't have to raid it for change as I've brought my wallet today, but I do have to think about supper as the bar closes. I've got a cool-box full of pasties and there's a microwave in the B&B so all is well on that front. When I plug in my trolley battery, laptop, mobile charger and GPS, the place begins to look like some kind of research lab with wires everywhere and half-eaten pasties on the laptop. I guess I have returned to being an untidy physicist for a day, both off the golf course and on it.

Millionaire's Golf on a Monday

Day 15: Thorney Park Golf Club with Mike K & Peter G. Sunny, light cloud. Shot 88 (29pts); walked 5.9 miles, lost 3 balls. Tight front 9, more spacious back 9.

There's something about golf on a Monday. Everybody's back in the office and there you are, out on the course—better than working! It's been quick to get here from my starting point by junction 13, but this is the busiest and most industrialised section of the M25, with 5 or more lanes each way. After flirting with Berkshire and a quick whizz back into Surrey, we're in and out of Greater London before we know it and apparently are now in Buckinghamshire; at least that's what it says in the club's address. However, we're not yet in the leafy lanes of Burnham Beeches: this is still very much West London.

I've got used to the comings and goings of Heathrow over the last few days and it's still only a couple of miles away. The course sits right next to the motorway, just north of the M4 junction and is hemmed in by the Great Western main line to the north and another railway line to the east, completing the triangle. You are surrounded by people going places, about their business and, to be honest, I was expecting a pretty noisy round. When I got to the club, however, all was quiet. Well OK you are aware of the motorway—it's only over the fence, but around the clubhouse, sitting on the terrace sipping coffee, looking over a reedy pond, you could imagine you were well into the country, which of course you once were!

There aren't many people about except the workmen setting out the new outdoor furniture on the terrace. Very nice. I think I've seen it somewhere before—yes, it was at Laleham on Saturday: they're sister clubs and have been upgrading their kit in one job lot. I get on with my pre-match routine, setting up banners, placing the sweetie-jar strategically at the bar, speaking to the staff etc. I even invest in a spare right-hand glove as they have a sale on. Start whenever you like, says the guy in the shop—we've very few people booked in today; it'll be millionaire's golf! Meanwhile, Mike and Peter have made it after a much longer journey from Kent.

I was nearly on my own again today. A mutual friend of Mike's had actually booked them both in at Stoke Park tomorrow and it was only a week or two before when I got an email from him saying he'd have to pull out on the 15th but Mike would still like to play. Hang on, I thought, I'm not there on the 15th, I'm here, so I let Mike know he could still play at Stoke Park but did he realise it was on the Tuesday? (I knew him anyway from my tennis club, but I hadn't known he was a golfer.) Oh, no, I can't do Tuesday, sorry: Monday's my last day of holiday and I'm back in the office on the 16th. Oh dear, two places to fill now at one of my top venues with only a fortnight to go . . . Fortunately Mervyn snapped one up, after his earlier experience at The London Club and apparently spread the word so effectively at the tennis club barbecue that not only did Mike say OK he'd play on the Monday but he'd bring someone else along as well. Peter, another regular on the court, is a very occasional golfer, but I'll help him round and he'll be fine, said Mike. Kamal had signed up too, but work got in the way a couple of days before, so in the end it'd be just the three of us, hitting a little white ball around the course rather than a soft yellow one across the net.

And it couldn't have been better. We saw hardly anybody on the course, which didn't help the charity collection at the bar, but, though close to the swish and rumble of trains and cars and planes going everywhere, we had time to stop and stare at ponds and streams

TREVOR SANDFORD

and spot woodpeckers in the trees as we went. This collection of real wildlife was soon joined by a menagerie of the golfing variety. Snakes, camels and frogs were frequently encountered and two gorrillas came out of nowhere to grab me on the 18th! Peter, nervous in front of an audience when one couple did eventually catch us up on the 11th tee, produced a number of contenders for pig, but made up for it all when, with unalloyed joy, he made his first par on the long 15th.

I stayed discreet about my own birdie on the same hole. I was playing rather wildly on the more spacious back nine anyway and didn't want to draw attention to the fact that I'd now played the 14th fairway *three* times—first by slicing off the 13th tee, then as it should be played off the 14th and finally with an enormous pull off the 15th which, a blind recovery into rough and a stone-dead 9 iron out of it later, yielded a birdie putt and the aforementioned 4! An amazing result which is becoming typical of my scrambling play when I consistently fail to find the fairway.

The whole day we had such a laugh, with no pressure and no one to please but ourselves, taking our time, enjoying and encouraging, bemoaning the bad and admiring the amazing. After the round, Mike gave me a cheque for what he would have paid at Stoke Park, which was about four times as much as today's green fee and more than made up for the rather slim pickings at the bar. He'd had a great day, relaxed, unhurried and just so much fun, and in fact it had been ideal for Peter to dust off the clubs and gain a bit of confidence in such an atmosphere. It epitomised two of the reasons we play the game—fun and friendship—and we had them both. It was worth every penny. Next time we meet up it'll be on the tennis court back home, but I bet it's the golf we talk about—that time in August we played millionaire's golf on a Monday.

Millionaire's golf

From film star service to ready meals

Day 16: Stoke Park with Jed, Mervyn & John A. Bright, windy. Shot 95 (27 pts); walked 7.4 miles, lost 1 ball. Too pretty to focus on the golf.

I had the biggest breakfast I've ever had at my B&B today but no wifi, so I head off early to Stoke Park. I'm not playing until the afternoon, but I might as well spend my time in elegant surroundings and with a full tummy I won't have to increase my mortgage to buy a sandwich at this exclusive venue. It's one of the "Big Four" on the tour where people are coughing up £100 to play; even that's less than the summer green fee, but the only other way I'd be likely to get to play here would be via some company golf day and unfortunately my sector just doesn't do that kind of thing.

The West London/home counties jigsaw continues today: we're in proper Bucks now, but surprisingly close to Slough, on which Betjeman famously invited "friendly bombs" to fall. My journey this morning has taken me through Windsor Great Park, past a polo club and on via a succession of offices any of which could have housed David Brent in his heyday. Turning northwards past the "Home of the Whopper" and two miles out of town we come to the country park well known as a corporate venue and frequently used as a film set. Scene of James Bond's famous victory over Goldfinger, it has provided a backdrop to many movies, adverts and promotions and it's not surprising when you pull up in front of what could be the best-looking clubhouse in the country.

A very pretty clubhouse

Oddly there isn't a serviced bag drop here, but you deposit your clubs before parking the car so as not to clutter up the front of the fine late 18th century mansion. Built with money received by John Penn in compensation for the loss of 26 million acres in the state of Pennsylvania, the transatlantic connection was there from the start and the club offers the Hollywood eye the archetypical image of an English country mansion. It has featured in Tomorrow Never Dies, Bridget Jones' Diary, Wimbledon, Bride and Prejudice and Layer Cake. However it is probably best known for the most memorable game of golf in cinema history with Sean Connery's 007 defeating Auric Goldfinger on the 18th, following a bit of cheating and ball-switching on the last (Bond deliberately missed the final putt giving away the win before "discovering" that his opponent had finished with the wrong ball and reclaiming victory). A display of posters in the locker rooms recalls that historic encounter and other movie memorabilia.

TREVOR SANDFORD

Still I can't wander about here all day as I have a blog to do, so I order coffee from the Orangerie and sit down at the business desk to get online. It seems incongruous to be looking at an Apple Mac on a Queen Anne table, but it works just as well and soon I've posted my piece about millionaire's golf on a Monday, no doubt influenced by surroundings used to hosting the real thing. This doesn't feel like the kind of place where my tacky sweetie-jar would look right and the manageress confirms that they don't do that sort of thing here. However, the barman is happy to look after it for me. When I've done, I wander out to the range where the pyramids of little white balls are sitting ready and I whack a few down towards the distant beeches. By this time, my playing partners are beginning to arrive, all the way from Essex and Kent. They've all played on the Golf Against Cancer tour before so they know what to expect, except today is a bit special and we have donned our trilbys to follow in 007's footsteps.

Half Way House

This time, however, there is no gamesmanship, crushed balls or flying bowler hats, just golf on perhaps the prettiest course we are going to visit. The camera comes out time and again to capture the scene and by the turn the sun has broken through. In fact I'm so distracted by my surroundings, my golf has actually gone to pot; Merv's illustrious play is keeping us in the match. At the halfway house I take a few commemorative photos as I realise, with some chagrin, that we are now exactly halfway through the tour. But at least the golf improves in the sunshine, despite the even greater distraction of the scenery: standing on the 16th tee, you could look in any direction and get the calendar shot of your life. I make a strong finish, missing the final putt just as Bond did in the movie, though, unlike him, I was trying to put it in.

Back in the bar, the guys in front, knowing we were playing for charity, gave us their match winnings—a tidy forty quid—but the sweetie jar was nowhere to be seen. I guess it just wasn't classy enough to be on display, but the waiter dug it out from under the bar where it had languished most of the day with the fiver I'd put in it to start it off this morning. Slightly embarrassed, he reached into what must have been the tip box and rattled in a few coins. Oh, no don't worry, I said, it's not *your* money I'm after! It was only whilst driving away that my disappointment was tempered as I realised why there wasn't any money in the jar. In a place like this you sit down, order your drink, the waiter goes off and gets it, leaves you the bill, takes off your credit card etc so nobody ever goes to the bar. The poor waiters must have thought I was trying to collect donations from them rather than their better endowed guests. I'm going to have to have a different strategy if I'm to make any money at places like this on the day, but the golf has done its bit and we have raised a total of £340, which isn't bad overall. In fact, I'm halfway round and a quick tot up tonight tells me I have £3,100 in the can already. At an average of £200/day, that's twice as much as I thought when I first dreamt up this crazy idea.

I'm off now to Berkhamsted, where I'll be staying for ten or twelve days in my friends' house whilst they're on holiday. It's well situated to reach all the courses on the north-western swing but I'll have to look after myself and that breakfast was now a long time ago. I drop into Tesco on the way and pick up a microwave meal as it's late and I've still got my day's admin to do: blogs, course reviews etc. Fingers on the netbook, fork in the pasta, I wondered if I should have pushed the boat out and got dinner in the Orangerie. I expect Bond sat down to a good lunch after his game, even though his host was furious after being tricked out of victory. I've come from film star service to self-service in a trice, from on stage to backstage. It was another great day and I've had a fabulous time in the idyllic environment I've left behind, but it is funny, you know, you never see them eat ready meals in the movies.

Signs of the times.

Day 17: *Northwood Golf Club with Graham N. Overcast. Shot 93 (29 pts); walked 6 miles, lost 2 balls. Rural calm in suburban setting*

I'm up with the lark in my home from home today as I have an early start, but encounter so little traffic going back down the M25 to junction 17 I get there in plenty of time. In fact I nearly drive past the place. Mindlessly following the Sat Nav, as you do, I suddenly come upon Northwood Golf Club right on the main A404 in the midst of suburban north-west London, and there it is, right on the street, with no apparent entrance bar a front door. I find a pedestrian gate for the pro-shop, but nowhere to drive in. This is most peculiar, I'm thinking, as I park on the road right outside the building. Locking the car I start to get worried as there is a sign on the lamppost which says:

POLICE NOTICE: EMPTY YOUR CAR WHEN YOU PARK IT—OR A THIEF MIGHT . . .

And I thought this was safe, suburban NW London; my brother-in-law lives a couple of miles away; my wife grew up here; I don't recall them saying it was a den of crime. Sign of the times, I guess. Anyway, the car's full of stuff—golf clubs, trolley, battery, spares of everything and a large crate that I now bring everywhere with change of clothing, balls, charity jars, caps, towel, plasters, ibuprofen, you name it. How am I going to get all that out? The main door is locked so I ring and Jenny lets me in. I feel like a tradesman and when she asks if I've found the car park I feel a right wally as it turns out I drove past it about 30 yards before. Thank you, SatNav.

Once parked inside this safe golfing haven and looking out over the course, I couldn't believe how rural it all felt, barely a lob wedge from the Queen's highway. The pro wasn't about but I was warmly welcomed with a coffee and a chat from the manager whilst I waited for my partner to arrive. Today I had actually cashed in my "You'll never walk alone" card and Graham was coming all the way from Maidstone to keep me company: midweek had, as before, proved harder to fill. Seeing we were a two-ball, the three seniors on the tee let us go ahead, light-heartedly reminding us of the expected pace of play. Hmm. Graham's still relatively new to golf and hates being rushed; let's hope we can hit it straight and keep ahead.

On the course we find undulating fairways and quite decent greens, giving the place a linksy feel though surrounded by parkland. We're pushing on to keep ahead of the blokes behind but after a while gain enough ground to relax and find ourselves quite away from it all: no traffic noise, no planes, just the birds tweeting. Later on we even come to what seems like a farm and all half a mile from the Metropolitan line.

The helpful signage continues: a small notice on the 9th tee announces: CAUTION, UNSTABLE BANK. So this is where Lehman Brothers have their golf days. Later, on the 15th, I nearly have to cut short my round when confronted by NO GOLFERS BEYOND THIS POINT. By this stage I have lost 4&3 to a 22 handicapper, so feel qualified to proceed. By the 18th fairway is a warning of DANGER: DEEP WATER but with the dry spring we've had it looks more like deep doo-doo. Fortunately I keep out of it. Indeed I'm having a bit of a lucky day on the course altogether, though I'm more of a billiard player than a golfer today . . .

I've overhit my second shot on the 9th and am on the 10th tee, while Graham is four feet from the pin in two. I'll mark my ball, he says, but for some reason I say, no don't bother and go for it with my lob wedge. Two bounces later my ball strikes his and cannons off at an angle towards the hole. In it goes for the luckiest birdie ever. It's even better than a chip-in, it's a chip-in-off! Graham sulks as he has to replace his ball and scrapes a par. He's driven for two hours to get here and this is how he gets treated! That's the second chip-in birdie in three days: all this golf is having some effect after all. As the saying goes, the more I practice, the luckier I get! It's a temporary moment of glory, however, as Graham walks off the winner in the end and I buy him lunch as a thank you for turning up.

After yesterday's low return in the sweetie-jar, I've given it more of a prominent position and I can hear some of the members pointing out the Cancer Research UK logo on my back as we sit out on the terrace and have lunch. That's the guy . . . playing golf for a month . . . the whole way round the M25 . . . yes I read about it in the paper . . . and he's here today? Etc, etc. Billie, an ebullient Irishman at the bar says I'd be better to leave the jar around for a day; where are you tomorrow, you could call back for it? As it happens, I'm at Moor Park about two miles away so I agree this time, as nothing has been nicked here so far and as long as I don't park on the road it all seems perfectly safe.

Graham's got to head off soon and I think again what a labour of love it has been to get here and back, as far away on the orbital as it's possible to get. But then he is a golf nut. We wonder which is the quicker way home—it must be about 50:50 from here. We call up traffic on Google maps on the smartphone and weigh up the options. Oh, I'll just go the way I came, he says. Some people will go a long way for a game of golf, or at least the second mile out of friendship.

The food is good but the atmosphere is somewhat subdued as there's a funeral party about to arrive: a lady member, apparently, well into her nineties. I'm conscious that nearly everyone I've met here is well over sixty: I suspect the younger members are at work, but I ask about the demography. It's a nice club, they say but we are struggling a bit to attract new members. When I get home and pick up the Berkhamsted Recorder, or whatever it is, I see that a local club at Boxmoor has had to close because membership was dwindling and they couldn't survive. In the 1970s I suspect there was a hefty waiting list at Northwood, as indeed there would have been in any club in a prosperous London suburb, but not today. It's the veterans and the visitors that keep things going midweek, otherwise they wouldn't survive either. There's another sign of the times I guess.

Can I go on?

High point of the tour in more ways than one

Day 18: Moor Park Golf Club with Steve C, Neil and Maqsood. Threatening rain fell in the end. Shot 86 (36pts); walked 6.3 miles, lost 1 ball. High Course proves a high point.

The forecast was for heavy rain, so I put my waterproofs on before getting in the car this morning, expecting it to come at any time. Another easy journey and I'm there in good time. Coming up the long drive past the public golf course, the road continues to rise ever nearer those dark, brooding clouds. Three hundred and sixty feet up—haven't been this high since Tyrell's Wood on Day 9. Then you swing round towards the magnificent Palladian mansion which is the clubhouse. I can see why this was the first venue on the tour to get booked up as Steve from my golf society, who works nearby, secured the spot for himself and a couple of colleagues way back in the spring. I don't know if they've looked at the weather forecast too, but I hope they've come prepared.

We meet up in the car park and just before we head inside I find a slightly worrying sign—I've become super-sensitive to these after yesterday—which says 3- or 4-BALLS ON THE WEST COURSE TODAY, 2-BALLS ONLY ON THE HIGH COURSE. Well I'm sure the west course is a perfectly fine specimen but we were really hoping to play the No1 track so now we have a quandary. The pro rings the green-keeper to check and yes, sorry that's how it is today, not exactly sure why. After a brief debate we decide to go 2 and 2 on the top layout. As a bonus it'll get us round quicker and we may even escape the rain, though it doesn't look likely!

Downstairs in the locker rooms, it's just as you'd expect in such a mansion. Reminiscent of Stoke Park or Walton Heath, there's a little boot room where you can leave your golf shoes on a named shelf and the steward will get them out for you, no doubt freshly cleaned. No time for such extravagance for us today as we head out to the High Course and get away. I play with Steve and Neil with Maqsood, but we agree on a matchplay pairs game. We are not playing together, so we'll keep the cards and go over them in the bar later. These guys are auditors and accountants, so they're used to scrutinising made-up figures after the event.

I'm not sure whether we played faster because we were a two-ball. It may have been that the first cut was quite generous so I didn't have to go wading into the rough to find my ball. Or maybe I'm actually turning that slice into a "power fade"? Well, I've had enough practice . . . I play the four par-5s in level par, which is always a good sign and finish up playing to my handicap with 43 shots on each nine. Not bad off the white tees where the Standard Scratch is 73 on a par 72. For the non-golfer, this translates as "I played well on a tough course." Maybe I'm over my worst now and ready for a good weekend; we shall see.

Today's chip-in birdie came at the par-4 seventh. Not from me this time, but from Steve who was absolutely delighted to get it in the hole from well off the green. We'll have won that one, we guessed, as we looked back to our opponents behind. It was a beautiful course with many lovely holes and my only complaint was at the quirky 11th where I lost a ball on a blind drive and ended up with a 7—I'd definitely play that one differently next time. It was dull and threatening all morning and, sure enough, on the 17th, the umbrellas at last came out. By the time we got back to the clubhouse, it was bucketing, but my freebie rainsuit survived this relatively brief test.

It got quite exciting going through the cards over a drink after. We relived each hole and felt the ebb and flow of matchplay as we marked up who'd won or lost. I've never actually done this before, but I'd do it again, just for the fun of it. Turns out we were 2 up on three occasions but, as often happens with accountants, in the end the figures came back into balance. All square at the last, even if a trifle damp. We'd all played well, Maqsood, the highest handicapper coming in with over 36 points. Not bad for a guy who hadn't eaten all day: it was Ramadan and whilst he was happy to chat whilst we had a drink, he slipped away discreetly before the food arrived—that would have been too much! Actually it was excellent—restaurant quality and really good value, quite surprising for such a grand venue.

Classy clubhouse

After coffee it was still pouring and I wasn't in a hurry to get away so I took a stroll around the magnificent building. Home in turn to Earls of Bedford, Pembroke and Monmouth, Moor Park has been closely woven into royal life for centuries, though the present house was built with *new money* made from South Sea speculation in the early 18th century. Then as now, no expense was spared in endowing the building with the trappings of gentility. The tromps d'oeuil and abundance of cherubs on walls and ceilings are more redolent of the Sistine chapel than a regular golf clubhouse. It was certainly proving a welcome host to a large Sikh family as they celebrated their wedding, the internal décor offering more than compensation for the weather outside. A high point for them in their lives today, as it was for us out on the course this morning.

Unsurprisingly, as this was not a day you'd have chosen for a casual round, the bar was pretty empty, so the charity jar didn't have a great day. However, I still had to go back to Northwood for yesterday's takings. Splashing my way down the A404, I made the quick round trip for its collection and was decently rewarded with the best bar takings since Ashford Manor. Maybe the funeral of a golfer helped to open the wallets in sympathy?

Back "home" I'm getting into quite a routine and I'm a bit behind with things so it's catch-up day with the admin. The checklist goes: reset SatNav, count cash, update collection jar total, charge battery, charge GPS watch, download photos to laptop, upload photos to website, write yesterday's blog, upload blog, scores and course review, write today's blog, upload etc etc. No wonder it's 9pm before I stop for a snack and then hit the sack. What day is it today? I haven't a clue. I think it's Thursday, but I have to check. You lose all track of days when you're on the road. It's like it was in my touring days in the band—another town, another gig. But this one has been a bit special. I put my score into the TSG website and find, hey, I've been cut! My handicap, having drifted up to a disappointing 13.8, is now back to 13.5—not enough to show on the card, but enough to give hope that the golf hasn't completely gone awol. It has been one of the high points of the tour so far: high quality in every way—golf, friendship, competition, food, culture. Where are we tomorrow—oh, it's The Grove. Fine. Bring it on.

This place has the X Factor

Day 19: *The Grove with Andy P, John O'C & Kevin T. Sunny.*
Shot 88 (34 pts); walked 8.3 miles, lost 0 balls. Lush fairways, slick
greens.

No surprise this date got booked up early on; we've all been looking forward to it for a long time. This exclusive venue with no members list plays host to the England football team before home games and its proximity to London makes it ideal as a celebrity getaway. From the moment you pull in at the bag drop, everything is taken care of. You have a coffee and return to find your car parked up and your clubs ready on the buggy. The pyramid of balls awaits on the practice range. On the first tee, the starter talks you through the buggy and if GPS is not for you, you help yourself to a strokesaver, then delve into the pile of tees, pitch repairers, whatever. All included in the price. It's Pay and Play, Jim, but not as we know it.

Coming out of the changing rooms I bump into a film crew setting up for a promotional video or something. Today I am accompanied by the galaxy of stars known as my playing partners. First is JO'C, who has already carried me to heroic defeat in two Ireland-England games. Then my regular pairs partner, Andy, with whom I have actually won stuff! We triumphed in the winter pairs at our club a year or two ago and made the final last year. As he's now the (nett) Club Champion, maybe I could play with him today? Then there's Kevin, a 10-handicap leftie with whom I've won the club greensomes twice! Spoiled for choice for partners today, but, ever loyal to my homeland, I settle for a third tilt at pretty formidable English opposition. I expect Hansen and

Lineker have the same dilemmas when they play here—or maybe they just throw the balls up?

John has done me a favour today. Since he knows in advance he'll be carrying me round, he's rung up in the week and asked for a buggy. Telling them it's my 19th day of golf on the trot and reminding them it's for charity, they've generously waived the fee so we sail around today in style. And what style! You pull up on the tee and say "what do we have here?" and a voice emerges from the screen giving you the complete low-down on the hole, pro's tip and all, and showing you the exact yardage to all points including today's pin position. Despite all this good advice you slice one off the tee and are heading for the rough. Not nearly as penal as the London Club, because before you get there, the buggy cuts out and a polite message invites you to return to the fairway. The buggy, guided by an eye in the sky, just won't go in the rough. The starter has explained the local rule which treats it like a hazard, allowing you to take a drop for a one-shot penalty and play on. We don't want those celebs dirtying their nice new Stromberg slacks by wading around in the long grass, now, do we?

The course is immaculate—"one of the best kept in Europe", according to Monty. I can play any club off the fairways and my Greens In Regulation statistics reflect this. It's like a US tour track. The greens are perfect, according to Tiger, but I took a while to find the pace (10.5 on the Stimpmeter today it said on the practice green, just so you know). Talking of Tiger, there's a neat plaque (one of three in fact) on the 10th fairway which reminds you that on Friday 29th September, 2006, at the World Golf Championship, he had 245 yards to go from here and, having made eagle the day before, fancied his chances of another. Hitting a 5-wood onto the green, he sunk the putt for the second eagle of the championships. "Do you think you could make it from here?" enquires the piece of slate. So out comes the 4-wood and I top it 100 yards! Oh well, the weather's perfect, I've had no excuse not to play well and I did: for the first time on the tour, I haven't lost a ball! I even get a chip-in birdie on the 14th, claiming to have laid up deliberately as it was easier than putting on those greens! On the downside, Ireland lost to England yet again. (Too near Wembley obviously; we'll get them at the rugby next weekend.)

Game over

Actually all this riding round in a buggy really isn't good for you. I forget how to walk and at one point feel an alarming twinge around the knee. Everybody worries about my abandoning the month of golf, but 800mg of Ibuprofen later I'm up and running, as it were and back on track. Not a good day for the sweetie-jar, however. I'd begin to feel embarrassed by it at these posh venues except no-one goes to the bar here and everyone pays by card; they are surprised if you offer cash and you don't dream of asking how much anything is. John is still reminding me what he paid for 3 coffees and a bacon roll! Could have got a round of golf in some places. Ah, but it wouldn't have been the same, would it?

I'm done now and everyone else has to get off, but I don't want to leave so I take a wander around the gardens, taking pictures of the many sculptures on display (you can buy a horse for £46,000 . . .) and taking a snap for some of the girls at the Hindu wedding in their fantastic colours. I ask a photographer to take a photo of me and we chat about how exclusive it all is. I wander round the corner and stumble on the film crew interviewing Gary Barlow on the terrace. A big guy who looks as if he might be in charge sees my camera and says "no photos during the interview". Fair enough I think and I listen in to the great man talk about his time in LA or whatever. My camera bleeps and I look down at it. A not so big guy who obviously is in charge ticks me off with "you've been asked once" before I have time to say "do you know who I am?" or anything, so, rather than spend the evening reminiscing with Gaz about our respective American tours, I head on back to pick up my kit. Twenty or thirty young X-Factor wannabees wander by, posing, pouting and trying to relax, hoping that this could be their stairway to stardom. They've had boot camp for a week at the Wembley Arena and are here today to find out who'll be their mentor for the show. Louis is probably in the bar and Kelly and Tulisa may be having a dip in the Jacuzzi. I'd join them myself but it's £205 a day just to go in and somehow at 6pm doesn't seem worth it, even for those two. I text my daughter who's well impressed by my recent encounters and make a note to tune in in the autumn just to see if I do appear in the background. Fame at last, Jim, though not as we know it.

Reverting to G-list celebrity status, I call for my car keys and hop on the buggy for a lift to the car park. It's only 100yards, but why walk when you can drive, eh? Suddenly I think: where are my clubs? I haven't seen them since I came off the 18th green. Oh, they're in the boot sir. Not used to this kind of treatment, I feel obliged to check and find a nice green jumper with The Ridge Golf Club on it. Must be John's, I think;

I'll take it back for him. But wait a minute, where's my brolly? Oh sorry Sir, we had to guess whose it was and we've obviously put it in your partner's car. Well that's fine but I'm on the road here, he's already halfway home, I won't see him again for a week and what if it rains tomorrow? Just a minute, Sir, he says and pops into the lost property, emerging with a nice "Ryder Cup at The Belfry" umbrella which looks like it was used once, if at all. Fine, thanks, that'll do nicely.

On the way home, I muse on the pros and cons of such attentive valet service. Being an independent-minded sort of person, I tend to prefer to look after my own things, but I must say it is nice to just sit back and let it all be done for you once in a while—provided they get it right in the end. I suspect I won't be coming here again in a hurry. Not that I wouldn't want to, you understand; I'd just make sure I wasn't paying the bill. But I've had a fabulous day and if yesterday was the high point on the tour, then this must have topped it. And the sun shone. They know how to keep you out here, but they know how to treat you when you're in. This place really does have the X-factor.

No driver needed at Berkhamsted

Day 20: Berkhamsted Golf Club with John A, Jeff and Steve S. Heavy rain clearing to sunny finish. Shot 86 (36 pts); walked 7.3 miles, lost 2 balls. Leave driver and sand wedge at home.

A weekend away from home and not playing until the afternoon, so why not get out and explore my adopted home? My friend Pete moved out here when the kids were heading for their teens and Hackney wasn't the trendy place it is now and you can see the attraction. This is a small town with *Quality of Life* stamped through it like a stick of rock. The main street has all the usual amenities plus a thriving farmers' market and the local branch of *Chez Gerard* is offering a free meal to anyone who got all A*s in their GCSEs! Nothing below B gets you a free pudding. There are plenty of nice-looking middle class kids around in just the right brand of jumpers. The supermarket just happens to be *Waitrose*, of course. I pop in to top up my supply of pasties and emerge with free range eggs, organic blueberries and Costa Rican coffee. It's half an hour by train to Euston which explains where the money comes from and the house prices in the estate agents' windows reflect that. This isn't grandiose affluent Surrey, just very nice middle class Hertfordshire. I could happily retire here, but I'd be living in a small flat. At least it'd be Edwardian.

I don't need a driver today—the course is just up the hill. I end up doing the journey twice as I have forgotten my wallet again. I need to go back for it as, for the first time on the tour, I have to fork out for the tee-time. Actually, it was difficult to get *anywhere* on a Saturday and the offer of 4for1 didn't seem too bad at the time. I'm sure if the secretary had been around we could probably have renegotiated, but that's another thing about weekend visits. The person who booked you in is not at work and there may just be a diary entry in the pro shop with something vague about cancer. As I wait for my three TSG partners to arrive I browse around the shop and snap up a very smart pair of Stromberg shorts—far too trendy for the people of Berkhamsted, so they're on the sale rail. I'll collect them after the round: I won't be wearing them today as it has started to rain quite heavily and people are rushing to get inside. Not looking good for the four of us then, as we gather by the first tee and decide to postpone the obligatory photo until later.

Dating from 1890, the course meanders through attractive heathland, well used by dog-walkers, mountain bikers and orienteers. Nearly all the par-4s run out of fairway at about 240 yards from the tee, so that's another reason I don't need a driver today. I don't need a sand wedge either as there are no bunkers, mounds and hollows protecting the greens instead. Maybe this'll be a day for the rescue club. Tell that to Jeff who refuses to hit anything other than the big dog whilst his lower handicap partner John sticks to a steady 5-iron. I team up with Steve, who has been to a driving range on his way here. Crikey, some people are taking this a bit seriously. In fact John and Jeff told me they signed up for TSG just to play with me on the GAC tour. Better up my game then; don't want to let the side down.

After a good number of pars on the front 9, we're 2 up and the rain has stopped. We've let a couple of 2-balls through already and we're on the 10th tee when suddenly my thumb goes. I mean it just goes; I can't even do a backswing. This is it folks, game over after 19½ rounds. Does anybody have a bandage or anything? No, why would they? Well obviously I'm stuffing in the Ibuprofen now and we're debating whether we continue or not and we're already looking at the clock when another 2-ball come up. Assuming they are members, we let them through, only to find that (a) they are also visitors who don't know their way round and are taking three shots to reach this par 3 green and (b) worse still, they're a fourball, as we see their other halves emerge from the hidden ladies' tee beyond. A five hour round is looming, with me walking in now. Jeff will have to ring the missus and renegotiate his day pass. And just to complicate things the pro pops out; everyone's gone home, he's locking up early and could he leave my stuff in the car?

So the guys tee off whilst I pop back to the car park and try to improvise a bandage out of a spare glove and a rubber band. Needless to say it doesn't last but I do manage to get off the tee with a rescue club more or less one-handed. Actually, that's not a bad shot and I par the hole. Swinging easy with minimal effort I par the next too and realise what I've been doing wrong all this time. Trying to murder the ball is never good for your golf and taking it easy is just the right medicine. Making myself do it is the hardest bit, but today I've no option and it works. I come in with nearly the same score as on the front 9 making 10 pars overall and not a bad total. Except we didn't actually play the holes in their proper sequence, cutting back a couple of times to get ahead of the slow group in front and making up the missed holes later. That'll blow the "miles walked" stats on the sweepstake. We even had time for a drink afterwards and the boys got back home in decent time to avoid any trouble. We still never persuaded Jeff off the driver but John's 5-iron was a thing of beauty. Despite that, however, Steve carried us to a 3&2 win.

On our way out, we saw the Berkhamsted Trophy honours board, recognising a few names from recent years. There's that Tom Lewis from Welwyn Garden City who led the Open after the first round this year. What did he score? 67,66—not bad. And who is that L Donald from Beaconsfield, back in his amateur days? By tour standards he's a short hitter but his accuracy with his irons has taken him to the top of the world rankings. This is a man who can have a driver wherever he wants to go these days, but I bet *he* didn't need one here either.

As I'm packing up in the car park, I get chatting to the solitary member who's still around. I don't know how it comes out but he's appalled that I've had to pay anything to play here, given what I'm doing and he'll write to the club captain about it. No worries, I say, it really is fine, I'm not complaining. We've had a good day and I've still raised over £160 pounds; I don't mind paying the odd green fee to keep the tour on the road. It's late now and I've got to get back to my blog and my blueberries, but lest I'm too healthy, I stop off for a Chinese along the way. I'm wondering now what to do about this thumb. Maybe Pete will have a bandage lying around the house somewhere. Or some kind of spray, or gel, or something or zzzzz. Yikes, I'm nodding off at the wheel now; thank goodness I've only got a mile or two to go, I'm so exhausted. Maybe I should have had a driver after all.

Heading home with a clear conscience

Day 21: *Aldenham Golf & Country Club with Ian M, Chris & Dave A. Bright and breezy. Shot 92 (28 pts); walked 6.7 miles, lost 2 balls. Start steady, open up later on.*

I'm cheating here today I think. Probably on three counts. First, Junction 21 doesn't really take you anywhere except onto another motorway. Second, today's club is much nearer the M1 than the M25. Third, and most serious, what am I going to do about Junction 21A? OK, it's only half a mile from Jn 21 and you'd hardly notice as you pass, but it's actually the one which links up to the quaintly named "North Orbital Road", the A 405, a fragment of the bits and pieces of bypasses that were scattered about London before the whole thing was brought together into one ring road. One junction or two, then? Well it's too late for debate as I turn off on this Sunday afternoon. I've been to confession in the morning so I'm sure all will be forgiven as I roll up to a very full car park. This place and The Grove are equidistant from the centre of Watford, but this I guess is where the locals turn out, a much more informal affair and a lot less money!

Maybe there'll be a bit more change for the collecting jar today then, but when I get to the bar I see that others have got there before me. There's the Captain's Charity jar, the Lady Captain's charity, Help the Heroes ... No room in the inn for another I fear. Well the barmaid says she'll have it but she can't really take the others away, so I'll settle for my place in the crowd and hope for the best. Joining me today first is Ian, the brains(?) behind *The Social Golfer*, bringing along his old marketing chum, Chris, who, curiously, calls him Bob and TSGer Dave from nearby Brookman's Park. I let Ian put up the Social Golfer banners today and we catch up on how the tour has been going and how TSGers have joined in. He is pleased that I have had company every day and most days have filled out completely via the website. The Essex stretch has been full for ages so the tour will have a solid finish, but it's been great so far, way better than I could have imagined.

How's the body holding up, he enquires, as he spots the strapping on my thumb. Oh fine, I say, but I have had a fair bit of support on the paramedical front today. It started with an innocent text to my mate Pete in Spain asking if he had any bandages in the house. I got an instant reply asking if everything was OK. Following my reassurance, he suggested I try Pete and Jo next door as they'd taken most of their first aid kit with them: he'd text the other Pete to let him know. Well moments later my neighbour in Berko appeared with the contents of his bathroom cabinet. Ibuprofen? Thanks, got that, lots of it. Some kind of cream, lint, gauze, an ominous-looking rubber glove, sticky tape . . . Now that might be useful, I conjecture, as I fashion a kind of thumb-brace out of Boots Padded Strapping Tape. Hmmm, yes, that feels good. Better still, it *looks* the part and will generate considerable sympathy on the tee as I have now discovered!

So off we go and out comes the rescue club for a bit of cautious straight hitting on the first few short but tight holes. I'm not playing great today but Ian's on form and we hold off the opposition nicely. Walking off the 12th after he'd won it with a par, I said "Well, that's 2/3 of the tour completed now" and he replied "well, you've got a 621 yard par-5 next!" The man has clearly no sympathy for the afflicted and I struggle on the unlucky 13th. However, I've played the five par-3s in 2 over, so it's not all bad, though coming in with 28 points, I forget all notions of having reached any kind of "plateau" where I can now play effortless, steady golf for the next ten days to the finish. We are definitely "coming down the stretch", as golfers peculiarly put it, and I'm going to have to look after myself with this dicky thumb for a day or two. A brief mention on the blog yesterday raises a flurry of emails almost amounting to national concern. Will he survive? Will he pack it in? Rory McIlroy hit a tree root yesterday and went off for an MRI scan on his wrist before deciding whether to continue to play, so I'm in good company. I suddenly wonder if my health insurance covers golf.

At the 19th hole I see that Help the Heroes has had a better day than Golf Against Cancer but I can't really quibble with that. Those guys are doing a great job and they should have our support. When I think what the average soldier goes through, I feel quite pampered in my gentle cruise around the motorway from club to club, niggly knees, dicky thumbs and all. By evening I've sunk into a hot bath and downed a very nice glass of wine from Pete's cellar. (Don't worry, I did top it up when I arrived.) Things aren't looking too bad and I pick up the old guitar we used to play in a band together in the 70s. Paul Simon's *Homeward Bound* comes to me with slightly amended lyrics. Maybe I'll do a karaoke version of it at the celebratory dinner on the last day—for a small fee—but, for now, here's verse 1:

> I'm sitting at a service station; I'm a long way from my destination, mm . . .
>
> On a tour of one-day stands, my golf clubs and guitar in hand
>
> Where every stop is neatly planned for a poet and a golfing-mad man . . .
>
> Homeward bound (I wish I was) homeward bound etc . . .

Really I think that wine has gone to my head. *Show me the way to go home* might be a better option, but I am definitely feeling I have "turned the corner" today and am heading home. I'm 21 down, 10 to go and drifting off down some imaginary fairway when I awake with a start and remember Junction 21A. What *am* I going to do about that? Can my conscience bear the sin of omission? Will I ever be forgiven? OK, here's the deal, says my inner angel. I see they have a nine hole second course at Aldenham: *next* time I go there, I'll play that as well. The quandary of Junction 21A now neatly resolved and parked well into the future, I let go at last and drift back into slumber.

Jewish club set for Christmas treat

Day 22: Dyrham Park Country Club with Kevin J. Sunny and warm. Shot 86 (35 pts); walked 6.3 miles, lost 1 ball. Tranquil parkland splendour.

You won't get a bacon butty at Dyrham Park: it's a Jewish club, opened in the 1930s when, shockingly now, Jews were unable to join other local clubs. Just down the road from South Mimms services, this magnificent Georgian mansion surrounded by tranquil parkland seems far removed from the world of commerce and industry that has no doubt sustained it with merely a handful of seniors and ladies about. Ah, of course, it's Monday morning again and with everyone back in the office, my friend Kevin starts his annual leave by joining me here. In the words of the poem *Linden Lea*, set to music by Vaughn Williams, which I have often sung: "Let other folk make money faster in the air of dark-roomed towns . . ." Today we are out in the park, the sun is shining, we've practically got the place to ourselves and are all set for a great day out.

The high Lexus count in the car park suggests they are not short of a few bob here and I notice the bag drop where the caddymaster is putting out trolleys for people. No need to pack up your stuff at the end of the round here—Jim'll take it indoors, charge up your battery and have it ready for your next visit. The same old-fashioned service continues upstairs in the locker room where, alongside the clothes brushes and the Brylcreem, a steward finds you a towel and sorts out your shoes for you. Who needs a bacon butty with this kind of service? The club does not take casual visitors but, curiously, societies are welcome so

I suppose Kev'n'Trev are the smallest society they are likely to get. I don't know why no-one else has signed up to day—oh, yes, I forgot, it's Monday!

A cloud appears on the scene on this otherwise perfect start to the day—my battery has packed up again. My repair job on Day 2 has lasted 20 days—that's more than three months of normal play, but only three weeks in the month of golf. I find the caddymaster and ask if he has a screwdriver. What's the problem, Sir? Oh, the battery connector, is it, well let me see what I've got in here. And out he comes with a battery which I'm welcome to use for the round, free of charge. Well, it'll be free of charge by the time I'm finished with it! So soon we're off and away as a very smart group of ladies let us go ahead on the first tee and a senior fourball in buggies are the only others we see, a hole or two ahead.

How do you describe one of the best days out on a golf course you've ever had. It's millionaire's golf again: hit the ball, take your time, enjoy the views, have a yarn. We play a match and I'm giving my mate half-a-dozen shots. I'm 2 down at the turn but the fun really begins at the 13th. Now Kevin, from our regular Saturday morning group, is an experienced trick-shot maker. One day on the 6th he managed to hit the ball at the tee-marker so that it bounced back over his head and into the rough behind. Today he goes one better. How he does it I do not know but somehow he gets so much backspin with his driver that the ball springs back off the turf and lands four feet behind the tee! In stitches, I tee up ready to take my turn and then realise: "Still you, Kev . . ." I wish I could have got it on video.

The fun continues and today's chip-in-birdie comes on the 16th. It's a short par-4 with trees and water on the left and I've hooked two down there already off the tee. The hazard is conveniently marked with a line of red paint along the grass and guess where I find my provisional—sitting right on top of it! Now we don't have a rule-book handy so we debate whether I'm in or out. I decide to play it as it lies and, teetering on tiptoe on the bank with my heels hovering above the water and my grip halfway down the club, I knock it forward to safety somewhere near the green—still provisional of course. On the way up we conclude that my first ball is definitely in the water; then Kevin notices a "Drop Zone." This means I can take a penalty for finding the water, drop one and play my third from here, rather than the now redundant fourth I've just taken. (Are you following this, non-golfers? There'll be a test after.) So out comes the lob wedge and up goes the ball, bouncing and bobbling its way up the green until—plop, in it goes for the most unlikely birdie I will ever get. A hook, a drop and a lob for a three squares up the match with my baffled partner and that's how it stays at the 18th to round off a terrific morning on the course.

Playing it as it lies

Back inside over a sausage sandwich, we decide we've had such a great time, we'll return in the autumn with the gang. Ismat in the office gives us all the low-down on winter golf deals but says that actually the Christmas special is always the most popular: tea/coffee and sausage baguette, 18 holes of golf and a 2-course Christmas dinner with all the

TREVOR SANDFORD

trimmings for £45. Sounds terrific. We take away the details and will talk to the boys about it in the autumn. Fair play, I think, for a Jewish club to be putting on a Christmas deal. That will amuse my Mancunian friend Colin with whom I'm playing tomorrow. Well, if it brings the money in . . .

Oh and didn't I mention the thumb? Well that's got to be good as I haven't really thought about it. The tablets/cream/tape combo seems to be holding it at bay. And you haven't asked about my feet. Thanks for asking, but they are fine. Two pairs of socks and the blister stick seems to be working too. It's just the battery that's letting me down now. Back in Berko I rummage through Pete's toolkit and find just the right spanner and pliers to do the business, so hopefully that'll keep me on the road for the final ten days or so. A quick call into *Boots* and I have enough tape to replace my neighbour's supply so I return the gauze and gloves with a free bottle of wine chucked in. Jo, answering the door, looks bemused; when did we keep wine in our first aid kit, she seems to be thinking. Well it's been in mine for most of the month and whilst I'm not yet ready to drink to success, I can manage to drink to excess, especially after such a good day at the office—or even away from it. It's another Monday, another great day out and now looking forward to Christmas. See you in December.

PS I am surfing through committee minutes on the internet and come across this entry about a membership proposal:

The genesis of the idea, due to Ron Omie, past President, to prevent a mass exodus from the club, was to offer members a special rate when joining in numbers: the motion was proposed by Levi Ticus, seconded by Joshua Schmidt and Ruth Cohen and passed by the committee, which judges it to have been a great success.

Apparently it mentions the first eight books of the bible. And you thought this was a book about golf . . .

In memory of Seve Ballesteros

Day 23: The Shire London with Colin, Barry L & Steve C. Wet, wet, wet . . . Shot 87 (35 pts); walked 8.5 miles, lost 1 ball. Risk/ reward: typical Seve track

There are few sportsmen who cast a shadow beyond their chosen domain onto life itself, but Severiano Ballesteros is surely one of them. An icon for many who grew up watching his swashbuckling style of golf in the 70s and 80s, he really put European golf on the map and has been such an inspiration to successful Ryder Cup and Seve Trophy teams. Latterly his course designs have captured some of the magic that the man himself displayed on the course, typically featuring the unusual combination of 6 par 3s, 4s and 5s, meaning no two consecutive holes are ever the same. On my recent holiday in Tenerife, my family could not understand why, when I was staying 2 miles from a golf course, I should want to drive nearly two hours to play another one. "But it's a Seve course" was my only defence and if I'm tried for hero-worship, I shall have to plead guilty.

And then he passed away in May 2011, after a long and courageous fight against a brain tumour which had first struck in October 2008. In that time he had established the Seve Ballesteros Foundation to contribute to research into brain cancer and it forms part of Cancer Research UK, so I'm already on the team. I'd probably have given all the money to the SBF if I'd been starting out now. At the Open Championship this year at Sandwich, you walked in through a corridor of pillars each displaying that iconic celebratory pose which has become the mark of a legend. Given the loss of his own wife from cancer, that would have helped inspire Darren Clarke to victory, I'm quite sure.

So there was no way a tour of the M25 could be complete without a visit to his first UK design. As it happens, Dyrham Park is nearer the junction but I played that yesterday and Old Fold Manor just across the road is closed for maintenance, so it's got to be The Shire today. Opened in 2007, it's a real risk/reward course where water features on 12 holes and you have to decide whether to play safe or "go the Seve route" on many occasions. Today has been booked up by three cricketing friends from Kent with whom I often play as a fourball. We have a range of handicaps amongst these occasional golfers so it's going to be a real test.

A greater test today, however, was simply getting out of bed. It's already pouring by 10 o'clock and the forecast says it's here to stay—what a contrast to yesterday's idyllic sunshine. No sane person would choose to go out on the course today and I half wonder whether my partners will make it as far as the Dartford crossing but I shouldn't have doubted the Teston *Rifles** as they turn up in good time ready for the challenge.

I've negotiated a discount today, but when I meet Tony, who owns the club, he won't have it and gives us courtesy of the course *and* a complimentary breakfast. We also get an enthusiastic tour of the gallery of Seve photos around the dining room, a pretty smart affair I have to say and get a couple of buggies at members' rate. There won't be too many people going out this morning so Pat, the starter, gives us his undivided attention, taking the banners off me to set them up on the course and giving advice on play at every turn.

We start with a tricky par-3 with water front and back so you just have to know your yardage and go for it. I've had plenty of practice and make the back of the green. 24-handicapper Barry thins one off the bank to get even closer. Steve and Colin find the water. Now not everyone appreciates an audience when their golf isn't quite their best and I can see that Pat's watchful eye and helpful remarks are not going down well with Colin. When is that bloke going to push off and let us get on with it, he mumbles? Hasn't he got work to do? I'm quite grateful, actually as he is still there on the third and helps me find my ball in the bushes, but by about the fifth his other duties take precedence over helping us hackers and Colin lights up a fag and starts to relax.

It's nice to have a buggy—only the third time on the tour—but it needs windscreen wipers. I keep wiping the screen with a spare towel so I can see where I'm going, it really is that bad. Colin's grumps have not helped his play and Barry and I are already 4-up after 5. I get into the groove and play 12-17 in level par and we reach the 18th with the game well over. It's a 419 yard par-4 and my mishit fade finds centre fairway with 192 to go. Now I have a club that is ideal for this in most circumstances, but the final green here lies within the sweep of a pond in the shape of a large letter S, in deference to its creator. Nothing but perfection will do. I could of course lay up with a wedge, lob onto the green and still make par. What would Seve do? Without hesitation, I reach for the 3-iron rescue club and to no-one's surprise it goes in the pond and I make triple-bogey. Like he says in the course guide, it's "a spectacular finishing hole that can easily ruin a good round".

So I've paid tribute to the great man by playing on through the rain and going for it on the 18th. Still, you have to, don't you? No one sits in the clubhouse boasting about their sensible lay-up on the last. Over a drink we scan the gallery of golfing greats looking on around us and I leave a note in the Book of Remembrance in the foyer:

Seve: I tried my best but you got me on the last.

Always a battler, always an inspiration, my golfing hero. Thanks for the memories. Severiano Ballesteros 1957-2011.

Rifle: one who takes the hard route where the easy one will do. A rifle will always "go for it", never lay-up. Much like Seve, really.

Why am I doing this?

Day 24: *Hadley Wood Golf Club with John O'C, Andy O, Peter E, Graham N, John A, Rod, Jack K and Dave A. Sunny. Shot 95 (28 pts); walked 6.2 miles, lost 1 ball. Nice course in posh area designed by Augusta man.*

It's August 24th and I'm beginning to get the feeling I used to get towards the end of the school holidays: back to reality soon, just another week of "living the dream". For the third day in a row now I get off at Junction 23 and down the A1081, sailing merrily past *Trotter's Bottom* and *Dancers Hill.* What quaint names the roads have in these parts: we are inside the M25 but it is very much "in the country" as you pass through Monken Hadley into Beech Hill. I could have gone another way but, drat, I've left the banners at The Shire. Pat did bring them in for me, but I obviously got so emotional signing the book of remembrance I just didn't see them sitting by the table yesterday.

So I roll up early and it's Ceri, the boss's son, who greets me today. Oh yes, you've left your stuff and, just a minute, I've got something for you. He rummages around the desk and comes up with a £100 cheque for Cancer Research, made out from the club. That's really generous, thanks, I say and we get talking about the Seve Foundation and the man himself and how many other courses around the world he's designed. About 60, is it? Now I can feel *two* months of golf coming on and Ceri says, great, he'll promote the tour. We exchange cards etc but I'm not even in the car park before the logistical issues start to arise. The great thing about this tour is that it's all nearby—you can actually do it all in a month without breaking the bank or damaging the ozone layer.

On past stockbroker mansions and we are soon at Hadley Wood which has proved a very popular venue with 9 of us lined up to play today. Hey I thought it was just a fourball every day, Trevor; this sounds more like a society booking. Well it has just grown. First of all, John is coming again. After three defeats by the English, I'll not force him to play with me again and he's bringing a couple of guys from his club too (as well as my umbrella, if you recall). Meanwhile another John has signed up and signed up in spades.

It was on my birthday (30th June) I got this nice present of an Email:

Hi Trevor:

You've inspired me to get my clubs out to join you for a 'Wild Week' of golf in Herts & Essex. 7 games in 7 days—am I mad or what?!! Here's payment for the games I've booked and I'm hoping to be able to raise additional funds. My cousin Janice sadly passed away 10 years ago after suffering cancer. She was 41. Without really wishing to give away my age(!), we were born in the same year. I'm doing this with her in my thoughts. Looking forward to meeting you,

John Amos.

He had only just joined *The Social Golfer* but noticed my project and signed up straight away for a whole week. With friends he was hoping to bring along, he could raise maybe £500? Great, John, welcome to the tour, so today is officially Day 1 of his Wild Week amongst the Month of Madness. Except that he's already had a couple of run-outs on Day 1 and 16 so we've got to know each other now and he's my unofficial No2 in the GAC fundraising department. Rod and Jack have come with him today and then I've got Dave again through TSG and Graham from Maidstone. People are coming back for more now: the month of madness is weaving its magic spell!

I was a trifle apprehensive about this venue after I read one review which said "Snobbish club with no community spirit" Yikes. Clearly we're in an affluent neighbourhood here and this is no cheap pay and play but will my experience bear out that comment? So far, not at all. Jane in the office has been great: they've already given me one tee-time but I ring up and say I've got 8 now and they say fine, bring 'em along. And only yesterday we were up to 9 so we can play as three 3-balls, no problem. I go upstairs to thank her before making my way to the pro-shop. Here there is a bit of confusion in the ranks about what the deal is, whether I'm supposed to pay, are we a society or what? These guys clearly don't read the Sunday Mirror, otherwise they'd know all about it.

I'm also reminded that private members' clubs which don't have to go out of their way to attract passing trade can be quite unused to having visitors around and knowing how to deal with them. However they've made a few statements already with the quite assertive sign on a tree saying CHANGING SHOES IN THE CAR PARK IS NOT PERMITTED and the rather more advisory : BEWARE SPRAYING GREENS. PLEASE DO NOT LICK YOUR GOLF BALL. I must say that's a bit more clear and polite than I've seen it elsewhere. Anyway, it's another very smart clubhouse in the Dyrham Park/Burhill style and the course is designed by Dr Alister MacKenzie, the creator of Augusta National so we are in for a treat. On top of that, they have the best practice nets I've ever used. Whether by accident or design, they are on a slight slope so when you've hit the ball it rolls back to you, saving you having to reach for another one. Nice.

On the course the teams go out as Kent, Essex and the TSG hybrids. Kent cleans up so at last JO'C manages to win something, even if it turns out to be a bottle of beer (he's normally a cider man!) "I'll treasure it", is his ironic indication that it is likely to remain unopened. Small takings at the rather quiet bar are more than made up for by the donations for golf and we make over £400 for Cancer Research UK today. Over a drink, Rod asks why I am doing this and, though I've got my back-story fairly well polished for the media by now I do wonder. Is it for a friend, a former colleague, a family member, or just for fun even? Before I hit the blog today, I really ought to have an answer.

Today it's for Melanie, his wife, Lady Captain of their club, who's going through chemotherapy. Yesterday it was for Seve. Tomorrow it'll be for someone else. It's for the 1 in 3 of us who may have to battle against this complex and often grim disease at some point in our lives. It's to increase their chances of being on the winning side. Today only 1 in 3 of us came out victors on the golf course. Let's hope that, in life, we can raise the odds a bit more than that.

Have I got enough balls?

Day 25: *The Hertfordshire with John A, John P, Kevin F, Ed M + 7 others. Very wet, clearing to sun. Shot 78 (42 pts); walked 6.2 miles, lost 0 balls. Good day out on a nice course.*

I wrote to both Titleist and Srixon before the tour to ask for ball sponsorship. I reckoned I could lose 100 balls in 31 days. Unfortunately neither felt able to help. Perhaps I should have tried Calloway, Nike, Bridgestone, whoever, run a beauty contest? Next time . . . Anyway I bought 8 dozen on special offer from Direct Golf; that should be enough, I thought. Some days I thought I'd need to restock; then at The Grove I didn't lose any. Could be the golf is actually improving—I've only had a couple of rounds in the nineties lately whereas that was the norm in the second week. Or maybe the courses here are a bit easier. Or perhaps I'm just learning to be conservative (some of the time). I look at my current supplies and reckon that, with a week to go now, I should be able to make it.

I've established the tradition that everyone who plays on the GAC tour gets a commemorative ball, hand engraved by yours truly with my own marker-pen, indicating the date on which they took part in the month of madness. It's part of the routine at the end of the game, over a drink: collect the money, take entries for the sweepstake, sign the balls. It's still on my conscience that I forgot to give them out on Day 1, but Ian and John will get theirs another day. So I do need plenty of stock, and today more than usual as there are so many people playing. In fact it's more of a golf day: I know that because we're having coffee and bacon rolls! My friend Ed whom I usually meet for wine-tastings organises an outing for friends and colleagues about this time of year and today he's come here to join me, bringing a few more hands to help me on my way. Kevin gets a lift up from Kent, John's here again from Essex with another friend and we have quite a party.

It's sunny as I pull up to the impressive manor house but the rain is due at any moment so I nip in quickly to find they are all expecting me. By this time I have got quite used to being recognised on arrival, or at least people saying "Oh yes, I read about you in the paper" or something but today I have an exceptional welcome. Elaine who organises the golf days is just determined to ensure we have a great time and nothing is too much trouble. Also, John's wife does floral displays here and has put a very tasteful arrangement in the hallway with notices about Golf Against Cancer alongside. We're all in a great mood as we munch our bacon rolls and talk about the tour so far.

Then we have to face the rain. Real, heavy, down-your-back stuff. Cover-your-trolley-with-a-plastic-sheet type of rain. Don't-even-go-to-the-putting-green type of rain. Will-be-lucky-if-I-score-well-today sort of rain. Even so it appears the Lady Captain has come down to see us off—that's beyond the call of duty—and she comes bearing a £50 cheque too! Chatting to Sue rather than face the downpour I learn that she's done her own golfing marathon—18 rounds in a day " . . . and I only had a buggy for 6 of them!" Thinking about this later, I can't quite believe it; it must have been a dawn-to-dusk effort with her practically running round the course. The things people do for charity . . .

We can't put it off any longer and brave the elements, Kevin and I taking on the two Johns in a Kent vs Essex encounter. Unlike The London Club or The Grove, the rough is all cut back here and you have a good chance of recovery if you miss the fairway. Ironically, I am hitting most of them today. A birdie at the 3rd follows and by the turn we are 5 up and the rain is starting to clear. I'm just short of the green at the par-3 11th but chip in for birdie! Just then, Elaine arrives in a buggy with a photographer from *The Mercury*. "Too late", I cry, "you've just missed it." My playing partners are relieved that he's after a still shot only so we settle for me picking the ball out of the hole; otherwise we'd have been there all day, trying to recapture the moment.

The magic continues as the sun shines. I get nearest the pin on the pretty 15th across a pond and make my third birdie of the day. By the finish I've shot 78, six below my handicap and quite the best round I've played all year, never mind the month of madness. In the clubhouse afterwards, people rapidly adjust their estimates of the number of shots I'll take over the month and the sweepstake benefits from a whole new set of entries. From today I'll stop posting my scores, just to keep it open, but will this round be the start of a final week of perfect golf, or just a blip in the stats? We shall see. And as for balls lost, I'm keeping that a secret now, though the answer today was zero.

Actually Ed's been pretty generous bringing all these other guys to play alongside the GAC tour today and it's a bit mean of me to run off with all the prizes. In the end most of the money ends up in the charity jar which, together with Elaine's efforts around the club, yield a very healthy £364 in all, knocking The Grove off second spot in the fundraising league table. However, I do end up getting the "big cheese" prize: it's a tradition that Ed's friend Quentin brings a nice piece of *Stitchelton* when he comes down from Leicestershire so my nearest the pin shot has netted that for me: it'll go down nicely with that old vine Zinfandel I've spotted in Pete's cellar, I say, knowing it'll make Ed's mouth water.

And it does, I reflect later, as I celebrate my final evening in Berkhamsted in style. I'll be returning home tomorrow with a pile of washing and a lower handicap—the TSG website has cut me by one shot after I entered today's super score. I'll miss a few things about this comfortable Edwardian house I've been looking after. Maybe not the shower though. Something about the water pressure means that if you want the shower to work on the top floor, you have to nip down to the first floor and get the shower there working first. Best to do this before you get undressed, I've discovered, as I flit past all those landing windows looking out towards the house opposite wondering what the neighbours are thinking.

Still I've survived a couple of weeks on the road, living out of a suitcase or sharing a house with an 18 year old heavy metal fan. It's been fun. I've eaten very few vegetables but lots of Cornish pasties. My back is fine, my feet are just about holding up and my thumb is OK for the moment, with the strapping continuing to elicit appropriate sympathy. But have I got enough balls, that is the question? To do 18 rounds in a day? Definitely not. But 31 rounds in 31 days? I'll let you know in a week's time. Or you could just ask the neighbours in Berkhamsted.

On the road, but have I enough balls?

TREVOR SANDFORD

Hips and shoulders,
knees and toes . . .

Day 26: *West Essex Golf Club with John A, Ian & Alan. Wet, wet, wet (again); walked 85 miles, lost no balls. Good value, quirky Braid design.*

Today I'm leaving Hertfordshire which has been my host for the past 10 days and entering Essex for the final stretch. I hope I haven't depleted Pete's cellar too much. I ask Henry what to do with the bedlinen, as I haven't time to wash it before I head off. Oh, just leave it, he suggests, which, as he's an 18-year old, means: my parents will deal with it when they get back. He's been good company for the ten days or so. I leave for "work" before he's up and he kindly turns down his music or goes out before I go to bed, so we've been very compatible house-mates. I've not made the most of Berko by visiting the Rex Cinema, so that will have to wait for another time, but I have enjoyed the *Waitrose* organic blueberries as an antidote to pork pies and pasties. I'm home tonight so I'm expecting to return to my normal diet of carrots and broccoli and getting my washing done, though to be fair, I have managed to keep the tour shirts washed and ready every day so I haven't completely slummed it on the road.

It's an early start today as I have a live interview on Radio Essex. The jungle drums of marketing have boomed ahead of me and Dave Monk wants to have a word on his morning show. We decide we can do it from the club, so I arrive early and find the office. It's already raining and looks set for the day, so I'll be happy to wait inside before we have to go. Emma greets me and agrees I can use her desk for the call when the time comes. I've done radio interviews many times and the routine is fairly predictable. Some back-room person rings you about 5 minutes before you are due on, puts you on hold listening to the show and then, after a brief warning, you're on live. If you have the radio on in the room you can even hear yourself with a slight echo which is very off-putting, so you don't! Thing is the office phones are busy and they can't guarantee the line will be free, so they'll call me on my mobile. I go to the bar to wait and mention this to the barmaid. Now she's very polite, but she's not in on the arrangement and says you can't normally use your mobile in the clubhouse. That's a fairly common house rule in golf clubs, but it could be a problem today. I look around and there's no one else in there, so I do wonder about the spirit and the letter of the law here. A bit more to-ing and fro-ing and somehow we eventually agree I'll take the call in the bar, so I even have to displace her from her workplace, but now she realises I'm some sort of minor celebrity, she is very accommodating and at the appointed hour, the call comes in.

Dave Monk, the morning show host, is the Essex equivalent of John Warnett, with whom I played on Day 3 and, though not much of a golfer, he's keen to talk about my Month of Madness on the M25, referring to me as "a man after my own heart", so we have a good bit of banter, I promote the cancer research cause, give a plug for *The Social Golfer* and generally loosen up for the day ahead. With the weather as it is, it's probably going to be the most enjoyable part of the day, and certainly the driest. Meanwhile my playing partners have arrived and we're surveying the scene outside over a coffee and talking about how it has all been going, their concerns clearly evoked by the protective strapping on my thumb.

Pain management in that department is now stable and that knee twinge that popped up at The Grove has not reappeared, so attention turns to other body parts. Two pairs of socks seem to be working on the feet and that blister prevention stick is a wonderful invention. Two gloves on the hands are working too, though I am getting an odd lump on my right ring finger. And the back isn't giving me much gyp these days. In fact, playing more golf seems to be healing—it is exercise, after all.

My thoughts are shared by my companions today. Alan seeks out a slope to run up and down to test out his new hip and John's friend Ian insists on hitting a 6-iron off every tee despite having done his shoulder recently in a motor-bike accident. I watch as he winces after every shot, but he says, no I'm sure it's not doing any damage, in fact it's making it stronger. I wonder if his doctor/physio would be in agreement, but I expect they have not been consulted. All the same, though, we swop Ibuprofen stories like serial drug-users.

Anyway, the rain's not going to clear so we'd better go and play golf. Off we set on an interesting, short but slightly quirky set-up that has you playing over hedges at various points and sometimes back over the green you've just come from. On the fifth tee we reckon we'd be able to see all over London—on a clear day! We're talking about focus and for a bet I say I can hit that puddle on this par-3 green with my 8-iron. I step up to hit and lo and behold, I do, but backspin for once drags me out of the water. This cocky sharpshooting could land me a chip-in-birdie today, John remarks, as the CIB has now become something of an expectation on the GAC tour.

So on the 7th, I make the bunker just short of the green and everyone else is on there, for one or a couple of shots. They go to mark their balls and I try the trick that worked so well with Graham on day 17. Just leave them there, guys, it'll give me more chance of an in-off. No way, they say, you'll just have to chip it in from the sand, and extremely wet, cloggy-looking sand it is today. So given no option after my previous display of accuracy, I swing, a clod of muck emerges with a ball in it somewhere; it splats on the green and out runs a little white object, straight into the hole! Today's CIB is a sandy one and the guys are wondering what I'm on. Can ibuprofen really have these kind of side-effects? I offer to run a workshop on "the role of luck in golf" at Tudor Park in September. That is, assuming the knees and toes are still up to it.

Putting away the clubs in the car, I see I still have a few of George's books, so I think today's efforts merit a prize. Not for myself, you understand, as I'm just doing an ordinary day at the office. It's Ian I'm impressed by. He's still wincing as he hits that 6-iron, but he's kept it up all day and turned in not a bad score: not quite enough to keep Alan and me from victory, but pretty close. So he gets the George Rothman award for playing through pain and is keen to come back another day. John presents me with something in return—page 28 of this month's *Golf International.* I've been thinking about that OB ruling, he says, and I picked up this at the club today. I'll have to take it home and look through it, I reflect, as I hit the road too late to miss the Friday evening rush-hour.

So it's back over the Dartford Crossing and into Kent. It's a Friday. It's 4.30. Any one of the previous three ingredients is a recipe for delay, but stir in all three and I'm definitely in for a slow journey home. Sorry, dear, don't put the broccoli on yet, I text ahead. Actually, I can't complain really. I've been on this road for 26 days now and I've only had very minor delays. I've never had to switch the engine off and get out a book. But today, as expected, I acquire intimate detailed knowledge of my dashboard and the back of the van in front as we edge our way southwards. Once released from the toll booths, it is only the normal "back home to Kent" commuter run, but I wouldn't fancy doing this every day. One time before, I just pulled off for dinner at Lakeside to let it happen and came home in the evening. But today the broccoli awaits and I'm sure I need the vitamin D as there has been so little sunshine to make my own lately.

Will I be welcomed home as hero or madman? Have I brought back too much washing? Should I have bought a souvenir? Has my beard grown too long? Will they recognise me? By now it's not "will I survive it?" but "*how* will I survive it?" and I'm sure, handy as it was in Berko, doing the final stretch from home will make it a lot easier. It will also be nice to have a shower without having to run naked downstairs. And—oh the joys of domestic bliss—I can even have a jacuzzi and soak away the strains on those shoulders, knees and toes.

Eat up your greens

Day 27: *Abridge Golf & Country Club with John A, Paul L & Tesh.*
Sunny intervals, showers. Shot 91 (30 pts); walked 6 miles, lost 2
balls. Lush fairways at Open qualifier.

Back in my own bed after a fortnight away, I resist the temptation of
an early rise for our normal Saturday 7.30am four-ball and have a good
lie-in. On such occasions I'd often treat myself to a fry-up or at least a
bacon butty, but today I'll give that a miss too. Why is the bacon roll
synonymous with the golf day? Where else do you eat ham, egg and
chips other than after a game of golf? How would I have survived the
month if I'd gone for the staple golfer's diet every day? I'd have needed
triple statins, if not a triple by-pass.

Week 1 was OK as I returned every day to my daughter's cooking as she
practised her recipes for survival at Uni. And very nice they were too:
her housemates don't know how lucky they are. Over the last couple of
weeks however, despite the civilising influence of the local Waitrose,
sharing a house with an 18-year-old whose sole diet consisted of pizza
has clearly been bad for the health. When I asked Henry if there was a
good takeaway locally he directed me to a "very good value Chinese"
where the spring rolls lasted me two days and probably contained a
month's recommended intake of sodium, let alone fat, nearly falling
through their soggy paper bag as a result.

Of course planning the games over mid-day means missing lunch and
I actually lost weight for the first week, but now I have the world's
supply of pasties, pork pies and flapjacks there is always food to hand

on the golf course. My wife is shocked, however, to hear that I have not seen a vegetable for two weeks. Well OK I did get a salad one day; does that count? So last night the conquering hero returned to a full three-course dinner, complete with carrots and broccoli! You know what they say about the way to a man's heart . . .

Today we have a leisurely start for our afternoon tee-time and I pick up Tesh from round the corner. It's half a month since I last saw him in Walton-on-Thames and he's amazed to see me looking so fit. Must be the no-veg diet! He was due to play tomorrow but, being a loyal Spurs fan, dropped out when he discovered it was a home match and moved to the Saturday. It's an Open qualifier course today, he says, so it must be good and it's nice to have a lift 'cos I can then have a cigar and a few beers whilst you're sorting out the banners and things. Thanks, mate, no problem, I'm well used to it now!

It's "will it rain, won't it rain?" as we check in at the clubhouse and have a coffee whilst we wait for the other guys to show up. There's a big society in ahead of us so I chat up the organiser who says he'll pass the jar round afterwards. John lives about two miles away but has never played here before and TSGer Paul makes up the fourball for another Kent vs Essex encounter. A heavy shower drenches us on the first tee but the rest of the day is pretty good weather. John gets off to a storming start and we're 3 down after 3. We've both made a pig's ear of the last hole and Tesh is feeling the pressure of playing on the GAC tour. When we stop to let a two-ball play through, John gives him a nice "calm down and enjoy it" talk. This somehow spurs me on to a birdie even though I haven't been listening!

On the second hole, John has played the shot of the week. From behind the pond on this par-3, he lobs the ball straight to the bottom of the cup, rattling the flag in its socket on the way. We all start to cheer this phenomenal chip-in-birdie until we remember it's only a par, as his first ball found the water and he's had to drop it for 2! Great shot, John—so near and yet so far . . . not a member of that exclusive CIB club yet, but plenty of chances to go. The fairways are so lush here, you can play any club with confidence and there's a good deal of banter about laying up short on purpose, just to get that elusive chip-in birdie, but it's not to be had today. On the back nine Tesh and I tidy up our game a bit and come off 1 up against the Essex boys.

I've had a look at that magazine article, I tell John, and I was right about the hazard ruling on day 22: good job I played the ball as it lay on top of the line, but it was redundant anyway as it was only a provisional. And what about that shot on the 8th at The Hertfordshire, you know when I moved the Out of Bounds post to play my ball as it was up against it? We never did get a ruling on that one, did we? We did get a ruling on the 8th today, though, and from the most unexpected source. I missed the green with my second and was up against some rather large but definitely staked trees. Normally you get a free drop when your swing is impeded by a staked tree, so I'm just agreeing that with John when my playing partner pipes up "It says here on the card NO FREE DROP IS TO BE TAKEN FROM ANY STAKED TREE—it's Local Rule No 11." Crikey, Tesh, where did you get that from? No one actually reads all that small print on the back of the card, do they? Well I had to do something while you were sorting out the banners. Thanks again, mate, you're a pal.

Fortunately Tesh is a great bloke and we get on well. Any over-zealous reading of the rules is long forgiven when he pars the 17th to give us the match. We both have a beer and collect up the banners together as we head off home after a great day out. *En route* I recount my adventures over the last few days, telling the tale of each chip-in-birdie as it happened and he collapses in stiches as the tales go on, convincing me they'd be worth putting down later for posterity, so I owe him one in the end. He's also paid double for his day out, so the charity collection is good too.

Four days left on the tour and I'm sure I'll be properly fed for the remainder. John's well into his wild week and still seeking that oh-so-special chip-in-birdie. For the next four days we are all going to be deliberately laying up short just to give ourselves a chance of glory. At home I'll be tucking into the broccoli, but on the course it's the lob wedge, not the putter, that'll be eating up the greens.

Month of Golf suspended due to disqualification . . .

Day 28: *Stapleford Abbotts Golf Club with John A, Greg & Murray. Wet 'n' wild. Shot 100 (22 pts); walked 6.6 miles, lost 5 balls. Not rushing to return, sorry.*

The Rules of Golf can be cruel sometimes—ask Padraig Harrington. For those who didn't follow the full story earlier in the year, here's an extract from *The Guardian* Sport section:

Chalk up another victory for the armchair vigilantes who today claimed the scalp of Padraig Harrington. The Irishman was disqualified from the Abu Dhabi Championship after an official, alerted by a television viewer, adjudged him to have broken the rules.

The original offence was minor—Harrington failed to replace his ball on the 7th green after inadvertently moving it a fraction in Thursday's opening round—but the consequences were unambiguous and the punishment was unforgiving. Having broken a rule, the player should have given himself a two-shot penalty. He did not, signing for a round of 65 when he should have signed for a 67.

Harrington will spend his Saturday hosting a golf clinic for kids and his sport will spend its time looking for someone to blame for yet another embarrassing rules imbroglio. In which case look no further than the R&A which, according to the rules official who disqualified Harrington, has been resisting a change to the Rules of Golf that would have saved the Irishman from his fate.

There have been other incidents, involving high-profile players such as Rory McIlroy, Ian Poulter and Colin Montgomerie. Three months later, the rule was changed whereby a penalty discovered *after the round* was imposed without disqualification. Peter Dawson, the Royal & Ancient chief executive, said: "For some time we have been concerned that, in certain limited circumstances, disproportionate disqualification penalties have been required by the rules. This carefully considered decision reflects our desire to ensure that the rules of golf remain fair and relevant in the changing environment in which the game is played today."

So all is fine in the world of professional golf and the armchair critics with slo-mo put back in their places. But surely none of this applies on the GAC tour—we're just a bunch of amateurs having fun and raising a few bob for charity. Well every golfer has his reputation to protect and I am a bit alarmed when I read further in the mag John has given me that you are not allowed to move an Out-of-Bounds post when it impedes your stroke. Don't ask me why: you can move a hazard stake or a distance marker or any other "moveable obstruction" but not the OB post, as it is actually "outside the course" or something.

I look again at my photo gallery showing my dilemma at The Hertfordshire. Not only was my ball probably out of bounds, but I have broken another rule by lifting the post to play it. My best round of the tour—indeed the year—now in tatters, surely the only thing I can do now is accept disqualification and spend the rest of the month in bed. Tempting, isn't it? And if I adjust my score it'll throw the sweepstake as well. The Month of Madness is ending in disaster, disgrace and expensive lawsuits. Well it's Sunday again, so I place my moral dilemma in the hands of a Higher Power. My recent experience suggests He must be a golfer and one with a very good sense of humour, given all the luck I've had on the course, so it is no surprise that my answer to prayer comes in this form: "post the photo on the internet, let the people judge and then carry on." So He's online as well? Well of course, He would be, wouldn't He? I was forgetting omnipresence.

The situation

The ruling

The red line de-
notes a water
hazard – but
can you deter-
mine which of
these three balls
is in or out of
the hazard?

A white line
always indi-
cates a bound-
ary – but could
you decide
which of the
three balls is in
or out of
bounds?

TREVOR SANDFORD

So I post the photo on *The Social Golfer* with the message: "If you can tell me that's definitely out-of-bounds, I'll call it a day. If you can't tell, I'll carry on" Well I suppose I am slightly interpreting divine inspiration here, as I haven't told them from what direction I took the photo, which rules official J Amos reminds me later in the day, but I get an instant response from "management" which says: "You're playing, leave the lawsuits to me." Whilst we're on, I suggest he clears the couple of slots he's been keeping for journalists on the last day and let John have one of them because, despite his avid research into the rules, he's been a terrific support over the past few days and should really be there at the finish. Fine, says Ian, I was thinking the same; I've got someone for one slot but he can have the other.

So, conscience clear again, I pootle back over to Essex, with Murray as driver. Stapleford Abbotts was described by Alan, with whom I played on Friday, as a "proper golf course", so I'm disappointed they don't have a strokesaver and have to rely on TSGer Greg to guide us round. Well maybe I'm just exhausted from my scruples or the toll is beginning to tell, but I'm struggling today. The extra length I've gained off the tee during the month is useless here with so many doglegs and without a course planner it's hard to know how far you have to hit the ball to get round the bend. On top of that, I've started to hook my "go to" rescue club. Five balls lost after five holes and I know it's not going to be a good day. Amazingly I par the next four, but it doesn't last and when the rain comes down in torrents on the 14th, John and I genuinely contemplate retirement. Poor lad's forgotten his overtrousers and his strides are sodden—and I'm in shorts! We press on but Kent loses today, despite Murray's superb chip-in-birdie on the 7th. Almost forgot to mention it, they've become such a regular feature on the tour.

Funny how you like the courses you play well on. The Grove and Moor Park will stay up there in my memory and The Hertfordshire will always be special, despite the rules controversy. I did like the Bernard Hunt course at Foxhills, but it was the treatment afterwards which made up for the golf. Today any criticism I have of the course is just a catalogue of excuses for poor play, but that won't stop me milking its faults when I next play with Alan—it's all part of the golfing banter. Even my 3-digit score today is a bit fictitious: in order to stop the "balls lost" rising to John Daly proportions (the former Open champion walked out of the Australian Open when he ran out of balls on the 11th), when I've lost 2, I put down a triple bogey and walk on; it doesn't happen much but it did twice today, on the 3rd and 5th. And I made a genuine 8 on the 4th in between. So not a good day at the office. But there is always tomorrow . . . and tomorrow . . . and tomorrow. After that I can give it all up—that is if I'm not disqualified first!

Getting up and down

Day 29: Romford Golf Club with John A, Ian & Paul L. Overcast Shot 85 (35 pts); walked 6.2 miles, lost no balls. Tight, varied, plenty of sand.

If it was difficult enough to get a tee-time at the weekend, then don't even ask about Bank Holiday Monday. Most clubs have some sort of members' competition, often with a shotgun start meaning the whole course is out of action for most of the day. As ever it has needed a bit of juggling so today I'm in Gidea Park, "the posh end of Romford" I am told, but well inside the M25 and feeling much like an easterly version of Ashford Manor. At least there's only one Romford, so people won't have difficulty getting there and they are all Essex men today, so I'm the only one crossing the river.

A traditional course in a flat, suburban area with little room to expand, the course defends itself by fairly tight drives, undulating greens, a few ponds and a great many bunkers. I counted 130, but on many occasions you drive back over the green you've just come from, so if you've missed them the first time, you can always have another go. Could be dangerous if the course is busy, I reckon, but we follow the members' competition at 3pm and have the place to ourselves into the evening. There are five of us today as John's father, Ron, joins us as caddy for a taste of the tour and Ian (of the bad shoulder) and Paul (from Saturday) are here for a second slice of the action.

We've done all the setting up, including leaving the collecting jar at the half-way house, which, curiously sits by the 11th tee. With all these members coming through, it'll give them a chance to find out about the tour whilst they sip their half-time tea. We can collect it there as we come through behind them, says the starter. We are a while getting away as we've waited for a photographer from the *Romford Recorder*. Jack takes a few snaps including a nice one of my practice swing which makes it onto the back page of the paper. John kindly points out later that the caption makes it look like I've had an airshot, but he's only trying to manipulate the sweepstake outcome now, having pitched in wide of the mark. I discover that my daughter's camera, which I've been using for a month, also has video so place it in Paul's safe hands to capture my swing. When I get home, I find a nice piece of footage beginning after I've hit the ball and stopping before the next one goes up. Oh, well, I guess I should have worked this all out a bit earlier.

On the course the bunkers aren't too fearsome if you plot your way around with the old rescue club. My game and Paul's are a bit up and down whilst John's is steady and Ian's still making good use of that 6-iron. We're 4 down with 5 to play and Paul puts a spurt on, birdieing the 15th in the conventional way. Still no CIB today, I'm afraid, John. However, we're inching our way back, thanks to my partner's play and still "dormie two down" on the par-3 17th. By this time the light is beginning to fade under grey skies but I nail my 7-iron onto the green. Paul's great run of play comes to an end with a duff off the tee. A few moments later, however, the impossible happens. From all of 75 yards out, he hits a wedge which bounces, rolls and runs right up into the cup, for the *longest* chip-in-birdie of the tour. We jump around, whooping and high-fiving, such is the cult status of this latest piece of fortune on the GAC tour, and there's nobody around to see us behave like kids who've just found the sweetie-jar!

Talking of which, it wasn't there when we reached the half-way hut. We did however find some cake, left by the lady members apparently. Oh well, fair swop maybe. However, once indoors we find it at the bar in the hands of Laurie, the Club Captain. First he writes out a cheque to

Cancer Research UK for £100 from the club and puts it in the jar, next he buys us all a drink and then he goes to join the tables where half the club, partners and all, are suited and frocked up for an evening dinner after their tournament. In place of the customary grace, he does a little speech about how there are mad people here today who've played golf non-stop for a month, look how much they've collected so far and we wouldn't want them to go away thinking we're the meanest club in Essex. Well said, mate, I thought, this could be a repeat of Ashford Manor in more ways than one and before we've finished our pints it comes back which what later proved to be a hefty £344! This, combined with the £105 already collected for the golf, knocks the aforementioned club into second place in the fundraising table. Great stuff, Laurie, we'll get that in the paper tomorrow too.

So we're coming towards the end on a high. Makes up for the low point of the day where, close to a pond as the summer evening drew in, I was beset by a swarm of midges and realised later that perhaps shorts were a bad choice of clothing today. I'm sure the wife will have some kind of cream for them, but by the morning the resultant scars elicit even more sympathy than the now-discarded thumb-brace. Oh, the ups and downs of a single day—and not one of them from a bunker.

There have of course been many other ups and downs—my weight for instance. It started about 75kg (sorry, you'll have to convert that into old money), then dropped to 73 after a week: can't have been my daughter's cooking; must have been lack of pasties. Now it's crept back up again; this time it *is* the home cooking—*plus* the pasties. Then there's the handicap. I'm playing now off what I was in June. I just had a good couple of rounds before the tour, got down to 12, have crept up to 14, and now back to unlucky 13 again. Mostly, though, I've been playing to about 18, shooting a daily average of around 90, as the clever entries in the sweepstake have noted. If only I'd been able to go round again, I'm sure I'd play so much better. Now, there's an idea!

So everything goes up and down and everything ends up more or less the same. Except that, borrowing from T S Eliot, you know yourself somewhat better, if not for the first time. You know the yardage for every club; you know what you *should* play off every tee. Whether the execution follows is another matter, as my round yesterday proved. And on that point, I have stopped posting my scores now, so as not to completely give the game away but, given so much info is publicly available, sweepstake entries are now doubled in price. The results will be revealed at the celebration dinner on Thursday evening, if I am still sober. You know Darren Clarke took about a week to get up and down after the Open, so I'll need at least a day to do the same.

What are you going to do next?

Day 30: *Thorndon Park Golf Club with John A, Kevin F & Jack S. Overcast. Shot 95 (26 pts); walked 6.6 miles, lost 2 balls. Challenging parkland setting.*

Weather a bit dull and gloomy today, and only 14 degrees. We got warmer days in November. Still, I'm into a routine here and just stick on the shorts on autopilot. That was my first mistake. The second was to follow Kevin's alternative route to the Dartford Crossing—would you take directions from a man who hits it backwards off the tee?! After an interesting tour of the industrial estates of North Kent, we finally emerge by the Dartford Hilton. At least we've avoided the traffic on the M2, he says, except today there wasn't that much of it: good shout for another day, Kev, I say.

I was to be accompanied today by the other Kevin from our Saturday morning group. As an Essex boy done good, he was keen to return to his roots and booked in for the last two days before his wife announced a change in the holiday plans. He got The Grove instead, which wasn't bad compensation, and freed up today for Kevin to continue his golfing week off. What trick-shots are we going to see today, Kev—maybe a chip-in-birdie?

John's here again and our fourth today is Jack from TSG. At least I think he'll be there. Apparently he lost a finger in an industrial accident about 3 weeks ago! Now I'm used to my partners having broken shoulders etc and I've given up pretending about my thumb, but losing a finger—surely that's enough to put the golf clubs in the garage for good? No, it'll be fine, says Jack's email; I've adjusted my grip and I can just about hit the ball OK. Well we shall see; or actually I'd rather not see, being somewhat of the squeamish type, if I'm honest.

We pull up at the "Wentworth of Essex" as Jack has described it and seek out Giles, the secretary, to introduce ourselves. Nice chap, old school tie . . . looks down at my bare knees, wondering if I've been sleeping rough by the look of all those gnat-bites, and says "no shorts in the clubhouse after 10am" but jokingly suggests that the pro would be most happy to sell me a pair of nice golfing trousers. "Good job we are out at 10 o'clock, then" I mumble, resenting the notion of shelling out on new Stromberg strides when I've got several perfectly good pairs at home and feeling a bit underdressed for the occasion. The "do you know who I am?" speech works a lot better with long trousers on, let me tell you.

Also this is only the second venue where I've had to part with cash for the tee-time. It's only £45 for us all, when the green fee is £50 a head, so I shouldn't grumble and if it's the Wentworth of Essex, it must be worth it. Oh and we wouldn't be keen on banners around the place either, by the way. But I've got a photographer coming from *The Advertiser*. Oh well you might like to do one on the putting green—most people do. And when I get out there I can see why. The practice green is practically the front lawn of Thorndon Hall, the Palladian mansion of which we are a neighbour and in whose original grounds no doubt the course lies. Handy backdrop that, a bit classier than a plastic banner I do have to admit.

By this stage I feel I have to make up for my lowly attire by bigging up our golfing credentials. Jack offers the fact that his Dad was once the greenkeeper here. I think *president* would be more the kind of thing they'd be looking for but we go inside for a pre-10am coffee and find a completely different mood amongst the other ranks. The kitchen staff have heard of our challenge and the chef wants to offer us a free breakfast. We've only time for a bacon butty but out it comes with a £20 donation for the charity jar. Things are looking up now and we head out full to tackle the course.

It's a good challenge, yielding no birdies today and few pars but we have an enjoyable game. Kent beats Essex 1 up but then Jack's playing with half a little finger on one hand and it's amazing he's able to grip the club at all, let alone play golf. Coming off the 17th I'm doing the score card and call across the green "How many, Jack?" He counts up on his fingers, as you do, and holds up his full hand for a five. "I'll put you down for a 4½ then!" He takes it well and has carried his quite significant injury with such an incredibly good humour that he definitely earns today's Rothman award for bravery on the course and goes away with a book.

Nearly done

John goes away with the photo of the month. We've stopped several times to let smaller groups through and, in the end, I just lie down on the turf with my feet up on the trolley, eyes shut, drifting away somewhere. John snaps it up and sends me a copy that night, posting it on TSG and it's the one the press will pick up on for sure in the "now it's all over" follow-up pieces after the tour. "M25 golfer misses last day due to exhaustion" could be the caption.

We slip back to the bar which is now empty and I squeeze in behind a table to cover up my scabby knees from view. Conversation turns to "What are you going to do next, then Trevor". Well, I'll go home, have a bath, something to eat . . . No, Trevor, *after* the Month of Golf, obviously. Oh, I'll probably go back to work—if I can get any! Actually I had thought of just carrying on. There are only 30 days in September, after all. It would be a shame to break the routine, now I've cracked it. But I've promised the family a holiday and I'm not bringing my clubs, so next week I'll be lounging by a pool somewhere in France I guess. Yes, but what about *next* year?

There have been a few ideas mooted—I've cycled from Land's End to John o'Groats in the past so why not do it with a golf club? Oh, it's been done before? Then what about all the counties of Ireland in a month (there are 32!), all the Seve courses in Europe (60) etc. But then I'd have to leave behind my dear old friend—the M25—who has been my constant companion throughout the month. I will miss her, but I do have that tribute chapter in the forthcoming book to look forward to. It's her 25th anniversary this year, you know, so worthy of special mention. Maybe if I get on with it, it could be in your Christmas stocking for 2012. There—that's the next project, then, but it won't be half as much fun as playing golf with you guys, and there'll be no chip-in birdies . . .

Turned out fine in the end

Day 31: Orsett Golf Club with Andy P, John A & Ian M. Overcast. Shot 89 (32 pts); walked 6.4 miles, lost 1 ball. Excellent course at welcoming club.

Now I'm sorting out my summer clothes and looking at my tan, to misquote Paul Simon again. When I did Land's End-John o'Groats on the bike I got "cyclist's tan". You know the sort—it stops abruptly half-way up your biceps and thighs; needs a good holiday after to even it up. This summer I haven't even got "golfer's tan". For the uninitiated, you can recognise this by looking at the hands. Normally the left hand wears a glove and stays white, whilst the right gets tanned (Other way round for Phil Mickelson *et al*), but Two-glove Trevor has two white mitts. Even the rest of me isn't very brown as frankly I haven't seen that much of the sun this August, despite being out of doors for 5 or 6 hours every day.

I have long believed that the British summer lasts from May to mid-July. When the schools break up, it all comes to an end. Here are my weather stats for the month of August 2011 to prove it:

11 sunny days (35%); 20 cloudy days (65%); 8 windy days (26%); 10 rainy days (32%).

So holidaying in South-East England, as I have been for the past month (!), you have a 1 in 3 chance of a sunny day, it's nearly as likely to rain and it's probably going to be quite cloudy, if not completely overcast.

No surprise the family are saying we need a holiday and playing golf doesn't count!

Over dinner last night the phone rang. It was Andy. What time have you got to be at Orsett tomorrow? Oh about 9, I suppose, but why do you ask? Cos I'm picking you up! Oh, that's great, but you know we have a fourball—me John, Ian and some journo friend of his. That's me, mate, he spoke to me last week. Sly old fox, that Mullins. Says we have some media guy and all the time he's holding a spot for my best mate. Nice touch. So I'll get to do my last sentimental journey on the hallowed M25 in the company of the guy who's kept it going all these years—and I get to play *with* my regular pairs partner at last instead of against him. What could be better on the final day of the tour?

Last time we were here on our recce, I had an enormous piece of cake, so this time I return to the Tee Bar for another helping. Bacon sarnie eat your heart out! The club is terrific—really welcoming: they've been kept in the picture by "PR" and everyone is looking out for the Man from the M25. The now-familiar questions spill out: "what was your favourite course, has you game improved with all that practice, how are the blisters?" etc. Miles the chef says he'll do me a lunch—I've a nice home-made pie if you fancy it. Deffo, but I need to walk off that cake first.

I met Steve, the Captain, on my last visit and he said he'd be around, so we do a few photos first and then he brings out half the committee to see us off on the first tee. No pressure, then. Of course I'm the first up, the fairway looks wide enough and BANG, we're away for the last round of the odyssey. I even find the middle of the fairway; in fact I find most of them today. It's gradually coming back together: Kent stay 1 up for hole after hole as I play bogey golf and watch everyone else get pars. Eventually I join them, though no-one chips in today, despite numerous near misses. Ian's having a stormer and it's really Andy's play that's keeping us in the game.

Nice course, Ian is saying, must do a review on TSG tonight. Don't worry, Ian I'm doing them every day. It's getting a bit tedious, though: I need a new way of saying it's a nice course. I was thinking Walton Heath is quite a masculine course, for instance, whist Stoke Park is rather feminine. So I could compare them to people perhaps? Well this is flat, but it's pretty and well looked after. Sounds about right, I think, as I set up to my pitch shot, banishing all thoughts of Keira Knightley from my brain.

On the 16th, Steve comes out to meet us in a buggy and follow us in. All square at the last, I hit a cracker on the fairway—and then find the greenside bunker. When we get closer, people start emerging onto the terrace, obviously primed for the arrival of greatness. I'm tempted to take off my hat and start waving, you know, like they do at the Open, coming up the last, but I still have to get out of that bunker. Fortunately I make it, but miss the putt for a final tally of . . . no, I'm not saying until tomorrow.

I guess I could claim a bit of distraction. We're approaching the green when all of a sudden a crowd of women in royal blue GAC shirts spring out from behind a bush with balloons and stuff—the WAGs have arrived! It's Diana and Heather, our respective other halves and my daughter Helena sporting a WELL DONE, YOU DID IT! placard. And there's Kevin taking photos of it all too, still enjoying his week off. What a surprise! A quick up and down (in 2), the terrace breaks into applause and we're all sipping champagne. Just like Darren at Sandwich. Miles serves up the lunch, the sweetie jar fills up and everyone goes away happy.

So that's it then. Month of Golf? Done, finished, surrounded by great people who've provided terrific support, as have so many others along the way, at clubs, through TSG, family and friends. I couldn't have done any of this without them: a BIG, BIG thank you from me. It's a dream come true and we've raised how much for Cancer Research? I'll let you know tomorrow, when all the stats will be revealed.

Meanwhile I forget that Andy's finishing par for 80 actually won the game, so we'll have to have a rematch at Tudor Park tomorrow. Yes, I've finished the month of madness and what am I going to do tomorrow?—play golf. Well I have made so many new golfing friends over the past month, I have invited them all to come and celebrate with me at my home club. It'll be a proper golf day, bacon rolls included. Score and sweepstake prizes will all be revealed and I shall basically just let my hair down, or what's left of it. If I shoot 100, get blisters and lose all my balls, who cares?

Then I'm taking the family to the south of France for a week—and *no* golf! Dave Monk on the radio had a go at me for going on holiday after my month's holiday, but that was tongue-in-cheek. It's been a fantastic month, exhausting but exciting, draining but dramatic. I wonder how much longer I really could have kept this going. Anyway, I need to do something about my tan. The weather hasn't been wonderful . . . but it's all turned out fine in the end.

We did it

TREVOR SANDFORD

Life After the Tour

And the winner is . . .

Day 32: *Marriott Tudor Park Golf & Country Club with about 20 others from TSG, friends etc. Wonderful, sunny and warm. Absence makes the heart grow fonder. Didn't keep score, don't know how many points I made, miles I walked or balls I lost.*

OK I know we are miles from the M25 here and the Month of Madness is finished, but just let me indulge myself here for a moment. I've met so many great people over the month I've just invited them all to my home club for a game and a knees-up afterwards. Most people are back at work but I'm prolonging the agony and so, it happens, are quite a few others as well, so I have twenty takers for my final fling back home in Bearsted.

It's September now, so of course the sun is shining, we have clear blue skies and it's not remotely autumnal as I roll up on Thursday mid-morning to a course I haven't played for over a month. I look at it through new eyes and it really does look pretty good. I'd have been quite happy to have turned up here any time in my month on the M25, it's as good as anywhere I've been. Or maybe it is just the weather? I've organised golf days in loads of places before but never here at my own club so it has been an interesting experience.

A great day out

People have been great. The office have given me a really good deal, as they know it's for charity and Brad, the Director of Golf, threw in a fourball voucher as a prize, no problem. Jason, the pro, gave me a couple of free lessons and Ann in the shop is giving me a buggy today—no charge. Actually, it's not a buggy I'm after, it's one of those three-wheelers, more like a racing trike really. First time I used one of them was at Buenavista, Seve's place in Tenerife, so one today will finish me off in style. I don't care what I score today, I'm just going to have fun.

Peter from the *Downs Mail* returns for his *third* photo-shoot for a follow-up article and there's quite a buzz around the first tee as we set off for the day. I drive us off and, on the spur of the moment, go for it left-handed with the driver. Actually, it's not a bad shot; I must try that more often! I pair up with Andy for a final Kent vs Essex match but

I've no idea of the score. I think we win, but it's not down to me. I'm buzzing round on the trike and just having a ball.

Actually I do get serious for one moment. On the 11th we have the longest drive and Andy has put a good one down. After a month of golf I have something to prove, so I tee up, pull the right foot back a bit and let rip. Down it goes, way past the bunker to a good 295 yards, dead in the middle of the fairway. I'm back! Bring on the winter pairs. It was rude of me to win my own prize but someone else gets nearest the pin and they'll all have a bottle of wine in the end, so nobody minds.

Everybody loves the course and says they'll come back again so that's a real bonus too. The boys from The Ridge are invincible today, but I must have a word with their Handicap Secretary after the comments I've had passed back to me—now that wouldn't be sour grapes from the Essex lads, would it? John is pipped to Nearest the Pin but drowns his sorrows with us as he's staying the night and doesn't have to drive back. Even the other John (of wrong Ashford fame) has managed to get to the right place today and Kevin's here again taking videos of the swings on the first tee.

Over dinner afterwards there are the obligatory speeches and I'm overwhelmed by the goodwill in the room, from people who've joined in and helped me live the dream. Ian presents me with a framed map of the M25 with all the stats on and Andy has come up with a complimentary massage for me here at Tudor Park and a "treat the wife for lunch" voucher to boot. We adjourn to the bar and celebrate a month that has been unbelievable, but fantastic fun.

And now for the stats. All scores now posted, I can reveal that in 31 days over 558 holes there were 2789 shots taken. Malcolm Jackson from Harrow got it right and wins a microlight flight. He's not even a golfer; he's one of my singing friends from Winchester, so well done to him. Several people guessed 2790, including Andy, who knows my game better than I do, and a certain Ian Mullins, who has clearly been looking at the TSG site. If only I'd 3-putted the last at Orsett . . . However, closest to the tie-breaking 211 miles walked and 57 balls lost were Dave Allchorne from Brookmans Park who wins a golf day for 4 at South Essex and Barry Frampton from Maidstone who gets another go at Tudor Park with a fourball. Hang on, says Dave, when I give him a ring the next day, is that the voucher we won in July and then donated to you for a prize? The very same, Dave. Well, put it in the auction or something; use it for the funds. I can't win it *twice*, can I?

I dig out my secret bet, hidden in my desk drawer and see that I'd guessed 2760. A bit optimistic, maybe, but only one shot a day off the pace. There are lots more stats, of course—miles driven (over 1500), pasties eaten (lost count), chip-in-birdies (6) etc. But the big winner of the tour is Cancer Research UK, where the money raised stands today at £7,725 (154% of target). That's many contributions from TSG members (including a staggering £1000 from John Amos and his supporters alone), golf clubs, friends, family and general passers-by.

I go home and in the morning, for the last time, update the blog, posting all the stats etc. The rest of the day is packing for France, re-acquainting myself with my children and just getting into the "do nothing" zone. It's hard not to keep running when you've been on the treadmill for so long. The site remains open at *www.justgiving.com/ monthofgolf2011* but it's now goodbye from me as I'm off to tackle the list of jobs my wife has kindly amassed for me over the month—but maybe they can wait until *after* the holiday!

TREVOR SANDFORD

So what do I do now?

Like I said, the easiest thing would have been to have kept going. Honestly! The hardest thing was stopping. I was a fidgety family member for a week on holiday in the Dordogne. Lying in the sun was hard to do; much easier to get out the map and go somewhere. Fortunately there was cycle racing on the telly so I could project my competitive urges onto someone else. Maybe that's why blokes tend to watch a lot of sport: it makes us feel like we are doing it, even if we aren't.

I did calm down eventually though and life did begin to return to some kind of normality. I still live with very minor celebrity in certain circles, fuelled by the continuing press coverage. The "he did it" story might not be as exciting as "he's going to do it" but it is more convincing. *Golf News, Kent and Essex Golfer* and the trusty *Downs Mail* all do their tale of the tour and the money raised gets up to the £8.5k mark, which is all good news.

I get in the *R&A Handbook* for 2011. No, I hadn't heard of it either. I'm on the page titled *Interesting Facts and Unusual Incidents* and they even give me a cartoon. I feature alongside university students who played up Ben Nevis during RAG week and octogenarians who are shooting ten-under their ages. Perhaps that will be my next personal challenge. And, of course, the 25th anniversary of the M25 causes a flurry of news reports around the end of October. I make *The Times* with a glowing report about how the M25 was my best friend etc. Very cheesy; hope Andy won't be too upset.

I do need to sort out my golf, however. It's all very well cavorting about the M25 for fun but I've got a few serious matches ahead and I mustn't let my partner down. The first test comes the day after we get back from holiday: it's the first round of the Matchplay Pairs and we're playing two 28-handicappers from a local club. Four down after 5, I mumble to Andy that we'll need birdies for a half as we're giving away a shot on nearly every hole and these guys are taking turns to par. Somehow, though, we scramble back into contention and nip it on the last. Phew—back to serious golfing reality.

I go and see Jason, our pro, for a couple of lessons to sort out that booming fade (polite word for slice) I have acquired and we make a few adjustments to get me back onto the short grass. We beat our club champion in another pairs match, so it must all be working again. Next year, I've decided, it'll be quality not quantity on the golfing front. I'm not going to go for the next marathon; I'll just try to improve my game.

By the end of the year I've played 125 rounds of golf. So has my game got better? Well I started the year on a handicap of 13.6 and have ended it on 12.7, so I suppose it has. However, I got down to 12.3 just before the Month of Madness, soared to 13.8 by the 24th and finished the month on 12.9, so I guess that means I got worse during that crazy month and I've only got better overall *despite* it! Conclusion: if you want to improve your golf, have lessons and practice, don't kill yourself on the course. Who knows, if I hadn't gone on the month of golf, I might have been playing off single figures!!

In December I fill in one of those online questionnaires about my golfing year. I'm astonished at how much I've spent over the past 12 months, even leaving out the month of madness. All those society events and visitor green-fees on top of golf club membership. Still, my average round has cost me less than 30 quid, and that includes 3 trips abroad, flights and all. If I leave those out, it's less than £20. Plus I have got a new electric trolley, fancy GPS watch, loads of spare balls . . . and lots of new friends as well as an unforgettable time on the road. It's been a great year, the best ever.

So what's it to be in 2012 then Trevor, they all keep asking? Well my cunning plan was 70 days of golf. No, seriously: here's the deal. Golf becomes an Olympic sport from 2016; the Olympics are in London in 2012—that's got to be an opportunity. The Olympic flame will travel the length and breadth of the country for 70 days, reaching within 10 miles of 95% of the population or something. What if all the golf clubs *en route* were to get involved and give a tee-time to charity and why not make it the Seve Ballesteros Foundation this time, in memory of the man himself.

I get into dialogue with the Foundation and even have the audacity to talk about "Following the flame for Seve" at the London Golf Show but then comes the bad news in an Email from Sophie at the SBF:

> *Unfortunately, anyone outside of the Olympic committee and the Olympic sponsors are unable to use the Olympics or piggy back onto anything they're doing at all. They . . . have asked us to advise our supporters, that an activity must not be seen to be using the Olympics in any way. Any activity seen to be doing so could be prosecuted! I know this all sounds quite extreme but I just wanted to let you know what we've been told!*

Yikes, I don't want the wrath of Seb Coe on me, I'm not a fast enough runner. Pity, though, I reckon I could have raised a five-figure sum at least. I'm pleased to learn that the SBF will be involving golf clubs in something else during 2012, but it won't be my project I'm afraid. I shall just have to *go* to the Olympics instead. (I did actually manage to get 2 tickets—for the Women's hockey, in fact . . . 8th and 9th place play-off, I think it was . . . gets more exciting by the minute, doesn't it?) Or maybe I'll be flopped on the sofa just watching, that is if I'm not down the range practising or having a lesson!

On a broader front, I've learnt what I already knew, that the game of golf, like anything you put yourself into, is a lesson in life. It gives you impossible challenges, but then you find a way through them. It puts you on the top step of the podium for a moment, but then cuts you right back down to size again. You know you haven't arrived and you never will. You know it's all about the journey.

And it's the same story with the M25. The road to nowhere, and yet the perfect parable for a golfing odyssey or indeed any challenge in life. It's not where you travel, it's how you travel, not who you meet but how you meet them, not what you're called but who you are. It may have been the Golf Against Cancer tour, but it has definitely been all about life.

GOLF AGAINST CANCER

A Month of Madness on the M25

M25

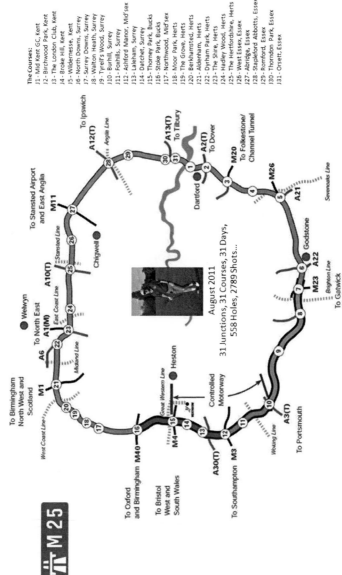

August 2011
31 Junctions, 31 Courses, 31 Days,
558 Holes, 2789 Shots...

The Courses:

J1 - Mid Kent GC, Kent
J2 - Birchwood Park, Kent
J3 - The London Club, Kent
J4 - Broke Hill, Kent
J5 - Wildernesse, Kent
J6 - North Downs, Surrey
J7 - Surrey Downs, Surrey
J8 - Walton Heath, Surrey
J9 - Tyrell's Wood, Surrey
J10 - Burhill, Surrey
J11 - Foxhills, Surrey
J12 - Ashford Manor, Mid'sex
J13 - Laleham, Surrey
J14 - Datchet, Surrey
J15 - Thorney Park, Bucks
J16 - Stoke Park, Bucks
J17 - Northwood, Mid'sex
J18 - Moor Park, Herts
J19 - The Grove, Herts
J20 - Berkhamsted, Herts
J21 - Aldenham, Herts
J22 - Dyrham Park, Herts
J23 - The Shire, Herts
J24 - Hadley Wood, Herts
J25 - The Hertfordshire, Herts
J26 - West Essex, Essex
J27 - Abridge, Essex
J28 - Stapleford Abbotts, Essex
J29 - Romford, Essex
J30 - Thorndon Park, Essex
J31 - Orsett, Essex

in aid of
CANCER RESEARCH UK

The **SocialGolfer.com**

GAC Tour Map

To Birmingham North West and Scotland
To North East
Welwyn
To Stansted Airport and East Anglia
To Ipswich
To Tilbury
To Dover
To Folkestone/Channel Tunnel
Chigwell
Dartford
Godstone
To Gatwick Airport
Heston
To Portsmouth
To Southampton
To Bristol West and South Wales
To Oxford and Birmingham

M1 M40 M11 M20 M26 M4 M3
A6 A1(M) A10(T) A12(T) A13(T) A2(T) A21 A22 A23 A3(T) A30(T)

West Coast Line
Midland Line
East Coast Line
Stansted Line
Anglia Line
Great Western Line
Woking Line
Brighton Line
Sevenoaks Line

Controlled Motorway

31* key definitions to help you penetrate the mysteries of golf

*There are actually more than 31 here, but that is just because golf is ever so complicated. In fact many of the terms used have two completely different meanings (see, for example, **club, hole** and **tee** below). However, a few minutes studying the following key terms should pay dividends in enabling you to enjoy reading this book despite having no interest whatsoever in golf. You might even be able to string a few of them together in a random way and give the impression you are a proper golfer. I have done this for many years and not been found out yet. Please note that the definitions below have not been approved by the R&A, USGA or any governing body of golf.

1. **Golf (n):** A game played with **clubs** whose purpose is to hit a ball into a **hole** in the ground in as few strokes as possible.

2. **Club (n):** (i) the stick with which you hit a golf ball, usually made up of a steel or graphite shaft and a clubhead made of steel **(iron)** or hollow metal **(wood).** (ii) the place where you go to play golf, or the organisation you belong to in order to play.

3. **Hole (n):** (i) the small circular dent in the ground into which you try to hit the ball. (ii) the whole area covered by the **tee, fairway** and **green:** there are usually 18 of these areas laid out in a sequence on a golf course, though sometimes there are only **nine. 19th hole(n):** this is not a hole at all, but is an alternative name for the bar to which players adjourn after a game to bore

other people with details of their **round** and possibly also to buy a **round**.

4.   **Iron(n):** any of the clubs with a solid metal bit on the end with a sloping **loft**; these are usually numbered 1,2,3 etc up to 9 as golfers generally can only count up to 9. **Iron(v):** what the wife does to your golf top before you play, if you are extremely lucky; you can do this yourself, of course, but I don't think I have ever seen anyone do it.

5.   **Wood(n):** (i) any of the long clubs with big, hollow heads designed to hit the ball a long distance, especially off the **tee**. (ii) where you have to go looking for the ball when it really should be on the **fairway**.

6.   **Tee (n):** (i) the section of each **hole** from which you start hitting the ball, usually off a **tee(ii)**. (ii) a small piece of wood or plastic with a sharp end which you stick in the ground on the **tee(i)** and a cupped end on which you place the ball before you **tee off(v)**. **Tee off(v):** (i) the act of placing the ball on the **tee** and hitting it (ii) the start of a game of golf, as in "we tee off at 9 o'clock" **Teed off, to be (v,t)** the feeling you get when you have played badly, are annoyed by your playing **partner** etc. **Tee shot(n):** the first shot from the **tee**. **Tee-time(n):** the time at which you are expected to start playing your round. (e.g. "I've got a 2 o'clock tee-time")

7.   **Partner(n):** the person with whom you play golf, but to whom you do not have to be married or in a civil partnership; in fact they might just be a **mate**.

8.   **Mate(n):** colloquial term for friend frequently used on the golf course, not necessarily someone to whom you are married or in a civil partnership but who nevertheless may be your **partner**.

9. **Fairway (n)** the strip of short grass between the **tee** and the **green** on which proper golfers generally try to land their **tee shot.**

10. **Green(n):** the very short grass surrounding the **hole** on which proper golfers try to land their ball in **regulation** prior to **putting.**

11. **Putt(v):** to strike a ball on the green, usually with a **putter. Putt(n):** the act of **putting** the ball. **Putter(n):** the **club** with a flat face usually used to **putt** the ball (e.g. the Ping Anser is a good putter"). (ii) the person who is **putting** the ball. (e.g. "Tiger Woods is a good putter")

12. **Rough(n):** the long grass down each side of the **fairway** where you definitely don't want to hit your ball.

13. **Out of Bounds(n):** the area outside the designated playing area of the hole, or course, marked either by the course boundary or by white posts or stakes. You definitely don't want to hit it there, as it'll cost you a **penalty.**

14. **Bunker(n):** a large crater-like hole lined with sand, of which there are many on a golf course (except odd ones like Berkhamsted) and where you generally don't want to hit you ball.

15. **Lake(n):** a picturesque expanse of water on a golf course which seems to have a magnetic attraction for golf balls.

16. **Penalty(n):** an extra shot or more which is added to your score if you break the **rules** or hit the ball **out of bounds** or into a **hazard.**

17. **Hazard(n):** the generic name for an area of the course including **bunkers,** streams and **lakes** where special conditions apply, such as not being able to **ground** your **club.**

18. **Ground(v):** the act of touching the **clubhead** on the ground when **addressing** the ball.

19. **Address(n):** the act of addressing the ball. **Address(v):** to stand with the clubhead behind the ball ready to hit it.

20. **Swing(n):** the act of pulling back the club (the "backswing") and moving it forward again (the "downswing") in order to hit the ball. **Swing(v):** to perform the said act, not necessarily in mixed company.

21. **Nine(n):** the sequence of **holes** played either first ("the front **nine**") or last ("the back **nine**") during the course of a **round.**

22. **Loft(n)** (i) the steepness of the slope on the clubhead which determines, at least for proper golfers, how high in the air the ball goes when struck. (ii) the place where you store your golf clubs between giving up the game and having grandchildren.

23. **Regulation(n):** (i) the expected number of strokes that a good golfer will take to from **tee** to **green,** leaving two more strokes to make **par.** (e.g. 2 on a par-4, 3 on a par-5). (ii) Some irritating and fiddly requirement made up by the governing body of the game which may or may not form part of the **rules of golf.**

24. **Par (n):** the expected number of strokes that a **scratch** golfer will take to complete (i) each hole or (ii) the complete course. **Par(v):** to play the hole in the expected number of strokes (e.g. "I parred the first hole" or "I parred the back nine").

25. **Round (n):** (i) the act of completing 18 holes of golf (e.g. I played a round with the boss's wife"). (ii) the number of drinks required such that each of your playing partners has one at the **19th hole.**

26. **Rules of golf(n):** an impenetrable set of conditions which must be applied by all who play the game of golf but which are understood by none of them and have to be interpreted even for the top **professionals** in tournaments by a **rules** official.

27. **Professional (n):** anyone who makes a living from golf, including people who play on **tour,** people who have passed exams and teach other people how to play and people who will sell you a bottle of water for £2.50 in the **pro-shop.**

28. **Pro-shop(n):** the place at a golf **club** where you book your **tee-time,** pay for your **round** and may also purchase golf clothing and equipment including bars of chocolate and drinks.

29. **Tour(n):** An organised sequence of tournaments or **matches,** often covering a particular geographical area (e.g. The European Tour, The Asian Tour, The Golf Against Cancer Tour)

30. **Match(n):** A game played between two or four players where one player, or pair, are the winners. Such games are referred to as matchplay singles or pairs **formats.**

31. **Format(n):** the type of game being played, e.g. strokeplay, Stableford or matchplay.

32. **Strokeplay(n):** the **format** where you count every shot you take until you finish the 18th hole.

33. **Stableford(n):** a **format** devised by the eponymous inventor to allow people to score on each hole, using their **handicap** allowance, taking into account the **stroke index** of each **hole**. (no, I don't think that's any clearer either)

34. **Handicap(n):** The number of strokes that you are expected to take to complete the course minus the number that a **scratch** golfer would be expected to take or, to put it another way, the number of strokes more that you are supposed to take compared to a **scratch** golfer, but I think that sounds complicated, so let's just stick to the first definition. (e,g, "I play off 12" or "I played to my handicap today") **Handicap(adj):** description of a golfer who is not as good as a **scratch** golfer.

35. **Scratch(adj):** the description of a golfer who has a handicap of zero, i.e. one who is expected to play the course in **par.**

36. **Stroke Index(n):** the rank order of difficulty of playing each hole, e.g. Stroke Index 1 would be the hardest hole on the course on which to make **par,** whilst Stroke Index 18 would be the easiest.

37. **Birdie(n):** a score of one under the par for a hole (e.g. a score of 3 is a birdie on a par 4). **Birdie(v):** the act of scoring a birdie(n).

38. **Eagle(n):** a score of two under par for the hole. **Eagle(v):** you've got it!

39. **Albatross(n):** three under par, but hey, who ever gets that?

40. **Bogey(n):** a score of one over the par for the hole. **Double bogey(n):** two over; **triple bogey(n):** duhh **Bogey(v):** come on, you must be getting the hang of this by now . . .

Games people play

There are many ways of playing golf—badly, for instance. In the month of golf I played strokeplay but often there was some other format running alongside. This is not a definitive list but here are a few different games you can play for up to four players. For some reason four is the usual maximum allowed to play together, otherwise it is just too slow, though we did witness a seven-ball on one occasion.

Strokeplay. Every shot counts and you are basically playing "against the course." You simply add up the shots taken and subtract your handicap from your **gross** score to give your **net** result. (e.g. An 85 playing off a 13 handicap leads to a net 72, which might just be **par for the course**). Often called **medal play** as this is the format used for the monthly medal competition at most clubs.

Stableford. This is complicated! You score *each hole* by working out your net score first (i.e. taking off a shot for each hole where the **Stroke Index** equals your handicap or less); then you score 1 point for a net bogey, 2 for a net par, 3 for a net birdie etc. (e.g. I make a birdie 3 at the stroke index 1 par 4, so my net score is a 2 (a net eagle) for four points, or "3 for 4"; a 19-handicapper would get 2 shots at this hole, so a birdie, if he managed it, would yield 5 points—"3 for 5"; however, he would be accused of banditry immediately). Why bother with this complication? Well, it means that if you get to the point where you can't score, you can simply pick up the ball and carry on, which speeds up play and it's more forgiving as you don't carry that bad score on your card as you would in medal play where one bad hole can be a "card-wrecker"

Matchplay. This is *mano a mano* where, in singles, scratch players simply play each hole to see who takes fewer shots. When you've won enough holes so you can't be beaten, you've won the game. (e.g. you may be "2up" with 1 hole to play, so you can't be caught. You've won "2&1". If you are 2 up with 2 to play, your opponent can level the match and this situation is quaintly titled "dormie" or "dormie 2". You only need to halve one of the remaining holes to win.) If you are "All Square" (i.e. equal) after 18 holes and there has to be a winner, you just start again at the first hole until someone gets ahead.

Handicap golfers play matchplay by "taking shots off the lower handicapper". E.g. a 10 handicapper plays a 14 handicapper: he has to give him 14-10=4 shots. These extra shots are taken on the 4 hardest holes, SI 1-4, to work out the net score. So if, say, the 14-handicapper scores a 5 on the SI 3 hole, it counts as a net 4 and would halve the hole with an opponent's 4.

In **matchplay pairs,** the **betterball** of the two counts towards the scoring, so if you mess up a hole at least your partner could win it for you. Shots are taken as in singles off the lowest handicapper, but as you are getting two chances here, you don't usually get the full allowance but ¾ of the difference (with 0.5 or more rounded up). Some people don't like this format as they say luck plays too great a part, but there's nothing better than taking turns with your partner to win holes, a process known as "dovetailing", clearly of carpentry origin. Betterball matchplay pairs is often called **Fourballs**, as there are four balls in play.

Foursomes. This is a 2-ball pairs format where each pair take turns to hit their ball. One player takes all the drives on the even holes, the other off the odd ones. This format is the most testing of any partnership; curiously, though, it is often played by couples and may or may not lead to divorce.

Greensomes. Like foursomes, except you choose which drive to take after you've played them.

Skins. The best net score on any hole wins a skin but it has to be an outright win. If it's shared the skin rolls forward to the next hole where an outright win will make two skins etc. so in all there are 18 skins to be won. If four people each put in 10p/hole, that's £7.20. If 10 people put in £100 a hole it's £18,000. It's up to you, really. Basically in this game you can play rubbish for 17 holes, hope everyone else halves them and then clean up on the last with a net birdie. Great.

The chair. Everybody takes shots off the lowest handicapper, as in matchplay. Basically if someone then wins a hole outright, they take on The Chair. They then score a point for each hole they win outright whilst occupying the chair. A half stops them winning a point, but they keep the chair. A loss means they are "dethroned". Complicated as it sounds, this is quite a good game for very mixed handicaps as everyone has a chance, though you end up with very small scores. You can vary it by successively increasing the tariff whilst in the chair etc. Alright, I give up, but I did play it twice and it worked OK.

Animals. A basic game in which anyone taking a 3-putt gains a **snake**, finding a bunker a **camel**, going into water a **frog** and out of bounds or in the woods a **gorilla**. A **pig** is gained by agreement for the worst shot so far. You can gain more than one of each animal but one is passed on to the latest person to win it, so it pays to be more careful towards the end of the round. You can put a price on each of the animals if you like.

Threesomes: useful if you have—you've guessed it—three players. Six points are distributed on each hole for the outcome of the net scores. The possibilities are 4-2-0, 4-1-1, 3-3-0, 3-2-1, 2-2-2 depending on how the net scores shape up. If everyone plays to their handicap each will win 36 points. The interest in the game is maintained even if you have no chance of winning, as you can keep someone else out, so may be open to bribery, corruption, side-betting and so on.

Texas Scramble. Everyone drives, then you pick the best drive and everyone plays again from there. Repeat the exercise until you hole out. This is a team game where each team of (usually) 4 plays against the others. Scores are usually low and the handicap allowance is something like 10% of the combined. You are expected to at least par the course and make a few birdies to win. Sometimes the number of drives which can be chosen from each player is restricted, to prevent you just taking the best person's shot off every tee. In the **Las Vegas Scramble,** you roll a dice after you have all driven and take the drive of player number 1-4 according to the outcome; a 5 or 6 allows you to choose the drive. This is a bit of fun really, but people play these kinds of game at odd times.

These are only a few of the many formats which can be played. We played most of them during the month of golf, but you can play whatever you like, provided you don't cheat. That is anathema to a golfer and sometimes you have to be dead careful not to cheat by mistake, e.g. by not knowing the rules. Having to explain all this to a non-golfer convinces me why I would never seek to write a book about golf, because trying to make it simple enough to be understood just seems to make it more complicated. In my experience, 99.999999% of golfers just want to have fun, get on with the game, get on with their mates and enjoy the camaraderie as well as the challenge. The other 0.0000001% just want to win at all costs, but I don't play with him any more. Enjoy your golf.

Make New Friends, Play more Golf!

The Social Golfer (TSG) is an internet golf community run and managed by people who are genuinely passionate about golf. Not simply another one of the all too common golf oriented "social networking" sites; The Social Golfer is a 'Real' social network, where you actually leave your PC and get out and meet people and of course, play more golf!

Originally conceived by a team of web developers based in Kent, UK in 2007, the site was subsequently taken over by Essex based golfer and TSG member Ian Mullins, in August 2010. At the time of going to print TSG had over 3,000+ registered users in the UK and 7,000+ worldwide.

The TSG community is a place where you can make new friends, join local golf games, run local golf societies and local golf groups, join in chat and forum discussions, track your scores, establish a Handicap (using both UK calculation and USGA calculation formats) and study your progress using our unique game analysis tools. You can also download your own official TSG Handicap Certificate (UK or USGA).

The site is designed to bring golfers of all levels together to meet up and play. The bespoke system allows you to track your golf handicap after every game and lets you compare your golf stats with your golfing friends/buddies/mates and compete in the monthly TSG league table. You can also upload your golfing photographs, share golf videos and catch up on BBC Golf News feeds for free and when you're not on the golf course, you can shop at the internet golf store, take advantage of green fee offers and source golf accommodation.

TSG lets you locate, read, review and rate over 25,000 worldwide golf courses and gather golf club information; such as green fees, scorecard details, Google maps and contact numbers.

Lastly, members can benefit from their fellow TSGers club members 'guest' rates and those rates negotiated by the TSG team. There are further discount deals on ticket offers, products and clothing.

With only approx. 31% of golfers in the UK belonging to a golf club, TSG are providing club members and non-club members with a great service that can only encourage more and more people to take up the game. In these times of austerity, we hope that we can keep the game both affordable and fun for those that already love the sport or only get to play occasionally.

The site is **FREE** to join and currently supports a number of charities including BALASA and Cancer Research UK.

Twitter: @*TSGers* - **Facebook:** *TheSocialGolfer.com* - **Linkedin:** *TheSocialGolfer*

Lightning Source UK Ltd.
Milton Keynes UK
UKOW050610180512

192793UK00003B/2/P